The New Complete Job Search

THE NEW COMPLETE JOB SEARCH

RICHARD H. BEATTY

John Wiley & Sons, Inc.

New York • Chichester • Brisbane • Toronto • Singapore

Copyright © 1992 by John Wiley & Sons, Inc.

All rights reserved. Published simultaneously in Canada.

This publication is designed to provide accurate and
authoritative information in regard to the subject
matter covered. It is sold with the understanding that
the publisher is not engaged in rendering legal, accounting,
or other professional service. If legal advice or other
expert assistance is required, the services of a competent
professional person should be sought. From a *Declaration
of Principles jointly adopted by a Committee of the
American Bar Association and a Committee of Publishers.*

Library of Congress Cataloging-in-Publication Data

Beatty, Richard H., 1939–
    The new complete job search / by Richard H. Beatty.
       p.   cm.
    Includes index.
    ISBN 0-471-53815-9 (cloth : acid-free paper)
    ISBN 0-471-53494-3 (paper : acid-free paper) :
       1. Job hunting.   2. Résumés (Employment).   3. Employment
    interviewing.   I. Title.
    HF5382.7.B445   1992
    650.14—dc20   91-41389
Printed and bound by Courier Companies, Inc.
Printed in the United States of America

10 9 8 7 6 5 4 3 2 1

*To those who are not simply in
search of a job, but are dedicated
to finding career happiness*

Acknowledgment

I would like to thank Richard M. Haviland, a friend and respected associate, who has made significant contributions to this book. In particular, his contributions to the chapters on preparing your predictive model and making the right employment decision were greatly appreciated and should prove extremely helpful to those who are intent on making the right job and career choice.

Preface

Too many job hunting books focus on only the "process" to be used in finding a job and completely miss the point. This author believes that the "real" purpose of job hunting is to find work that is professionally and personally satisfying, a work environment that will allow individuals to achieve their full potential, and a work experience that produces a sense of gratification and fulfillment—in a word, to find "happiness" in the work place.

Persons who simply go in search of a job will find that—"a job." Individuals with a sense of vision and a desire for an improved state-of-being, however, will seize the opportunity presented by the job search to enhance the quality of their lives. This means not just becoming familiar with the mechanics of a good search process, but also taking the time to truly understand what it is in a job and work environment that is important to achieving job satisfaction and happiness. That is what this book is about.

This book is much broader than the typical book on job hunting. It provides a logical, step-by-step process for conducting an effective job hunting campaign. In addition, it provides the reader with some excellent methods for evaluating specific job opportunities against known criteria that are important to the job seeker's own personal satisfaction and overall happiness. Specifically, the reader is taught how to construct and use a personal "predictive model," that will allow him or her to better understand themselves and "predict, with a high degree of accuracy, the type of job and organization that will best match their own profile and maximize their opportunity for success and career fulfillment.

This book also leads the reader through a highly systematic, step-by-step process for conducting an efficient and hard-hitting job hunting campaign. In this sense, the book represents a very complete job hunting manual covering all of the important steps of the job hunting process (in actual sequence) including preparing a personal "predictive model," defining the job objective, picking the right resume format, resume writing, key employment sources and how to use them (14 of them), the direct mail campaign, the employment networking process (by which some 70 percent of all jobs are found), techniques and strategies for winning the interview, how to make the "right" employment decision (using a "predictive model"), and how to effectively negotiate the job offer. It is all here!

The advice and counsel provided in this book are the result of this author's more than 25 years of first-hand experience in the human resources, employment, and outplacement consulting fields. This includes nearly 18 years as a human resources executive with Scott Paper Company and nearly 8 years in the human resources consulting field. During this time, I have been involved first-hand with the employment, placement, and job search counseling of hundreds of individuals in a wide range of jobs and organizations. Additionally, as a leading author in the field of job search (7 books including 2 bestsellers), I have appeared on *Good Morning America,* and have been quoted on job search and employment matters in hundreds of publications across the country. Also, I serve on the Boards of two not-for-profit educational institutions concerned with the professional training and certification of career consultants and employment professionals.

This book has been written to serve the novice and seasoned job seeker alike. I firmly believe that, if you carefully follow the step-by-step process outlined here, the odds are greatly in your favor that you will be highly successful in conducting an efficient job search that will result in finding not only a job but also a satisfying and rewarding career.

Best wishes to you as you launch your job search and begin to write a new chapter in your life. Hopefully this book will, in some way, help you to make it an exciting and rewarding one!

RICHARD H. BEATTY

West Chester, Pennsylvania
March 1992

Contents

The New
Complete
Job Search

1

An Introduction to Job Search

If you are going to run an effective job hunting campaign, there is an inescapable logic to the steps and sequence of the elements of the job search process. Failure to understand this basic principle can add several unwanted months to your overall campaign.

Each step in the job hunting process is an important prerequisite and preface to the next. In many ways, it resembles the construction of a building. You must first start with the excavation, then the foundation, then the first course of blocks, and so on, until the structure is complete. You are the architect, the engineer, the contractor, and the laborer. Should you lack the necessary skills to do the work, or should you omit any of the basic steps, the structure can be weakened and crumble in a heap with the first windstorm.

Job search is much the same way. It must start with the excavation (that is, digging through your past and your current life experience to discover and understand the type of work and organizational environments that have proven satisfying), proceed with the foundation (setting a target job objective), and then move to each subsequent stage of the construction process (the steps of the search process), until the structure is complete. Lack of specific job hunting skills or failure to follow the critical steps of the process will result in a substantially prolonged job search or a fatal flaw that will undermine the entire process and jeopardize the end result (that is, your career).

Since most of us spend better than 50 percent of our waking lives performing our jobs (or in job-related activities), finding the right job and employer can have a very significant impact on the quality of our lives. Job search failures can be devastating to both ourselves and to the ones around us. The stress and unhappiness that is created by a poor employment decision affects not only our working lives, but has a way of spilling over into our personal lives as well.

Importantly, much of our self-esteem is associated with how we feel about our contributions and impact in our work environments. Successful performance on the job can do much to affect our feelings of value and self-worth. Conversely, poor job performance and lack of compatibility with the organizational culture of the employer for whom we work, can significantly contribute to a sense of worthlessness and low self-esteem.

Numerous studies have shown that there is a high degree of correlation between one's mental state and their overall health. Job-related stress and unhappiness is known to be a key contributing factor to serious, and sometimes fatal, medical conditions. One usually needs to look no further than their own family to see first-hand examples of this fact.

So, the job hunting process should not be taken lightly. There is simply too much to lose. Life is simply too short not to enjoy what we are doing to make a living.

The start of a job hunting process presents you with a major opportunity to put a number of things "right" in your life. You should therefore not waste this opportunity. This is a process well worth taking the time and effort to do well.

Prepare then to do some hard work and to commit the energy and resources to do it well. This is not a time to look for shortcuts or easy ways out. Yes, job search is a process that requires a good deal of discipline and hard work, but the end result (i.e., your personal well-being and happiness) are well worth the momentary sacrifice that you will need to make. So do it well!

This book will provide you with a step-by-step process for finding a satisfying and rewarding job. Each step is presented in a planned sequence which, if followed, should automatically result in the creation and execution of a highly effective job hunting campaign. Each step is critical to the final outcome of the search process.

The first step of the job hunting campaign, defined in Chapter 2, provides for the development of a "predictive model," which helps you to predict, with a high degree of validity, the type of job and organizational culture needed to maximize your effectiveness and achieve a high level of job and career satisfaction. Since this is the ultimate objective of any good job search process, and the entire process needs to be focused to this end, it makes sense that this should be the very first step in the job hunting process. It is the centerpiece and focal point for all of the rest of your job hunting activities.

Chapter 2 therefore provides you with a series of practical self assessment exercises that will help you to profile the kind of job and organization that is a good match for your knowledge, skills, and personal attributes. The net result of this chapter will be the preparation of a personal "predictive model," that can be used to measure and predict the probability of a good match between your own profile and that of the employers you may wish to consider.

Chapter 3 then provides the next logical step in the job search process. It provides a process to help you to define a specific job objective or definition of the target job that you will wish to pursue.

Having defined your job objective, you are then ready to prepare the employment resume. The subject of resume preparation, a critical component of any job hunting campaign, is covered in depth in Chapters 4 through 8. In order to increase appreciation for the difference between a good resume and a poor one, Chapter 4 provides samples of both. This is then followed by instructions on resume selection, advance preparation, and actual resume composition. Several resume samples are available in this section for your review and reference.

A well-written resume is clearly essential to launching your job hunting effort. With this document in hand, you are prepared to contact employment sources and begin your actual campaign. A prime aspect of the search process at this point is knowing what employment sources to contact, and how to efficiently use them. Chapter 9 identifies some 14 key employment sources, and is packed full of valuable information on how to effectively use them.

Two methods employed in most successful job searches are the direct mail campaign and the employment networking process. Because of their importance, Chapters 10 and 11 have been devoted exclusively to them. The "how to" approach used in these chapters should make it fairly easy for you to learn to effectively apply both of these techniques.

With these key employment sources and methods in full swing, it will be just a matter of time before some job leads develop and your efforts land that first all-important interview. Don't leave the interview to chance. Make sure you are well prepared! Chapter 12, *Interview Power: How to Win the Interview*, deals with not only how to prepare for the employment interview, but also provides specific interview strategies which you can use to gain significant competitive advantage.

Chapter 13 also deals with the subject of interviewing. Here a number of key questions are presented which you will need to explore during the course of your interview discussions. Answers to these important questions will provide you with certain data that will be critical to making an intelligent, informed employment decision.

Chapter 13 is also concerned with helping you to make the "right" employment decision. To accomplish this vital task, you are provided with a series of exercises that will help you to profile both the work and the culture of the target organization, resulting in the construction of an "organizational model" which describes, in detail, the characteristics of both. By comparing this "organizational model" with your personal "predictive model" (developed in Chapter 2), you are provided with a powerful tool for taking much of the guesswork out of the employment decision process and arriving at an objective and well-founded conclusion.

Successful interviews lead to job offers and negotiations. What are the best strategies for negotiation success? How does one prepare? What are some of the most effective techniques? These and related topics are the subject of the final chapter, *Negotiating the Job Offer.*

As you can see, each of the chapter topics presented in this book is an integral part of the overall job search process. You will need to become intimately familiar with each if you are going to conduct a well-planned and successful job hunting campaign. The step-by-step process presented here, however, should facilitate this process and stack the deck in your favor for a favorable result.

Let's now move to that first step of the process.

2

Preparing Your "Predictive Model"

Considering the fact that you spend between 60 percent and 70 percent of your waking life either at work or in work-related activities, selection of the right job and company is obviously a critical event in ensuring your general happiness and well-being. Unfortunately, most people simply jump off into their job search giving little real thought to those factors that are essential to their personal satisfaction and tranquility. And, the results are too often disastrous.

The beginning of a new job search should be viewed as opening a new door to your life. It offers you one of those rare lifetime opportunities to "put a number of things right." It provides you with the chance to find work that is personally and professionally satisfying and also to find the kind of work environment in which you will flourish and experience a sense of inner peace and contentment. The resultant sense of happiness and well-being can spill over into your personal life and provide

6

you with a feeling of fulfillment, positive self-image, and overall harmony.

The problem with most job searches is that people tend to focus on finding a "job." Seldom do they stop to think about those elements of a job and work environment that are truly important to their personal satisfaction and positive motivation. The result is, they spend a good part of their life doing work they dislike or working in an organization in which they are uncomfortable.

Such circumstances are unfortunate and take a real toll, in terms of the quality of their lives. Not only is their happiness affected but, in some cases, it threatens their very life as well. It is no secret that work-related stress and anxiety are major contributors to not only mental depression but also to several life-threatening diseases including fatal heart attacks.

As one who survived a heart attack at age 40 and quadruple bypass surgery at age 52, let me say that life is too short not to enjoy what you are doing! If you have not enjoyed your work-life previously, it's time to get it right and to put in place those things that are truly important to your overall happiness and well-being. You have the rest of your life to look forward to. Why not do it right? This is your chance to do so!

WHERE DO I START?

The answer is simple. You start at the beginning!

The real beginning of the job search is with *yourself*. This is a time for some real self-searching and introspection. If you don't first understand yourself, there is little chance that you will be able to identify and select the kinds of employment opportunities that will prove satisfying and rewarding. You simply have no criteria against which to evaluate and judge whether both the work and the culture of an organization are going to be a good match for those factors that will be important to your personal motivation and general contentment.

It is the purpose of this chapter to help you to systematically examine yourself—to better identify and understand those *job* traits and characteristics that must be present to ensure your satisfaction—and to identify and understand those *organizational* traits and characteristics that are essential to your happiness and sense of "fitting in." The resultant profile is what we term the *predictive model,* and can be used by you to better predict the probability for a successful employment marriage.

A WORD ABOUT CULTURE

Unfortunately the employment interviewing and selection process, from both the candidates and employer's side, tends to be heavily "job" focused. By this I mean that both parties tend to primarily focus on whether or not the candidate can perform the job. Little meaningful thought is typically given to the other critical dimension of the employment process—organizational culture (whether or not the candidate will "fit" and be happy in the work environment). Yet, this is one of the most critical factors in the employment equation. Whether or not you feel comfortable in the work environment will impact your motivation, productivity, and overall happiness. This is not an area that should be left to chance!

Over the years, various studies have clearly shown that one of the critical elements to having a successful employment experience is alignment with organizational culture. Perhaps as much as 80 percent of all employment failures are, in fact, the direct result of such misfit.

A small survey of outplacement consultants that I conducted two years ago, shows that somewhere between 70 and 92 percent of all executive and managerial "firings" have little or nothing to do with technical competency, but are instead the result of lack of "fit" with organizational culture. As a person who has spent more than 25 years in the human resources profession, I was not particularly surprised at these findings. I had long believed this to be the case.

I have seen it happen repeatedly. Both parties (candidate and employer) are so focused on the job, and whether or not the candidate has the technical knowledge and skills to perform the job, that they forget to look at the broader issue of whether or not the candidate will fit the organization. Perhaps neither party is to blame since, in my judgement, the human resources profession has done little to train and equip people with the ability to make such a determination. The result is that this critical area is frequently ignored by both sides until after the candidate is hired and it is already too late! We have all seen this happen.

In psychological terms, what is happening is that the candidate does not align well with the basic "value system" and "behavioral norms" of the organization. What the candidate "believes and values" is not the same as what the organization "believes and values." Since what a person believes and values drives the way they tend to behave once inside the organization, a candidate whose value system does not align well with that of the organization will tend to behave differently than his or her counterparts. Such "inappropriate" behavior is quickly evident to the organization, and the candidate is seen as "not fitting in."

Taken to the extreme, misalignment with organizational culture can have dire consequences. If you do not align well with the value system and behavioral norms of the organization, you will soon be labeled as a "misfit" and rendered ineffective. Because you have different values than those of the rest of the organization, it will be difficult for you to get support for your ideas. Those who wield decision-making power in the organization will view your ideas as "strange" and withhold their personal support and the resources that will be necessary for your ideas to succeed. Thus, you are doomed to performance failure.

As a human resources professional, I have seen this scenario play out time-and-time again. Sooner or later, the hiring manager goes to the human resources manager to complain that good old Jim is simply "not working out." He is a "loner," "keeps to himself," is "not a team player," is "uncooperative," is "not doing what is expected of him," "is not getting the important things done," and so on. Shortly thereafter (following some performance discussions and a half-hearted attempt at a performance improvement plan, of course) good old Jim is terminated for "poor performance."

Interestingly, although these terminations are frequently labeled as "performance" terminations, such employee firings seldom have anything at all to do with technical competence (that is, having the specialized knowledge and ability to successfully perform the job). Instead, because the employee does not align well with the culture of the organization—the organization's value system and behavior norms, the reality is that the employee is never even given a "chance" to perform. All support is withheld, and the employee is labeled a "performance disaster."

To further my point about the importance of cultural fit, consider the following. What constitutes "highly desirable" behavior in one organization, can be seen as "totally unacceptable" behavior in another.

For example, a young, fast-growing, highly entrepreneurial organization may tend to value individuals who are "decisive, action-oriented, risk-takers, who can rely on their intuition and make quick decisions." Persons with these traits will tend to fit in and will be perceived as "successful" in such organizations.

By contrast, the *very same* characteristics may spell unmitigated disaster in a mature company in a slow-growth industry, where preferred behavior may emphasize such traits and characteristics as "detailed analysis, thoroughness, conservative decision-making," and so on.

You can see that the very same person (with the exact same level of knowledge, skills and abilities) will be a roaring success in one culture and a total disaster in another. Thus, cultural fit plays an extremely critical role in a successful employment marriage. Without it, you are dooming yourself to a lot of unnecessary unhappiness and the potential for a major derailment of your career.

In this chapter, we will help you to take an intelligent look at this matter of cultural fit and will provide you with a process that will enable you to identify those organizational traits and characteristics that will be important to predicting the success of your impending employment marriage.

You will be wise to heed my advice on this subject and give equal balance to both "Job" and "organizational" fit when making your final employment decision. It is now important to introduce you to "predictive modeling."

THE PREDICTIVE MODEL

Our purpose is to help you to avoid the major pitfalls of the job search process by helping you to prepare a "predictive model" as the basis for conducting a successful job hunting campaign. This model, if well-constructed, will allow you to evaluate prospective employment opportunities (on the basis of your own profile) more objectively and predict the probability of a successful match.

The predictive model is a model that depicts the ideal job and organization that is best suited to you. It describes those job/organizational traits and characteristics that must be present in both the work and work environment to ensure your motivation and personal satisfaction. In general, it is intended to provide you with a solid basis for predicting the likelihood of a successful job and organizational match, and to ensure your happiness in a prospective position.

Successful development and application of the predictive model, as an effective job search tool, is dependent upon the careful execution of four basic steps. These are:

1. Developing a *"self-profile"* (your likes, dislikes, motivators).

2. Conversion of your self-profile into a *"predictive model"* (the type of job/organizational culture you best fit).

3. Development of an *"organizational profile"* (a descriptive job/cultural profile of a specific employment opportunity you wish to consider).

4. *Comparison* of your "predictive model" to the "organizational profile" to predict the probability of a successful employment match.

By profiling the ideal job and organization (the predictive model) right from the start of your job search, you will be much better prepared to compare this predictive model with the profile of organizations and job opportunities you may wish to consider along the way, and arrive at an intelligent decision that optimizes your chances of job satisfaction, career success, and happiness.

The balance of this chapter will lead you systematically, step-by-step, through the predictive modeling process. To facilitate this process, you will be led through a series of exercises—first, to enable you to develop a "self profile"—and second, to translate this self-profile into a "predictive model" of the type of job and organization that will be an optimal match for your personal skills, traits, and characteristics. By doing so, you will have put in place a vital component that should prove critical to the ultimate success of your employment effort.

DEVELOPING YOUR SELF-PROFILE

In 1978, William Crockett of National Training Laboratories developed a concept known as "Managing the Critical Three." This has proven an invaluable, easy-to-understand tool for use by job hunters in ferreting out the components of a job that are important to successful performance.

According to Crockett, all jobs can be divided into three core parts, known as the "Critical 3." These core parts are:

1. Task Management

2. Self-Management

3. Interpersonal Relationships.

Each of these core job parts, with a little guidance, can be described in terms of identifiable activities and attributes. And, all three of these job parts are interdependent (dependent upon one another) because of the way work actually gets performed in an organization.

Thus, for you to be able to construct your own personal profile and measure how well it may (or may not) align with a given job opportunity, you must first understand not only the "job tasks" that must be performed but also the "organizational climate" in which the work is performed as well.

The entire process, however, must begin with understanding yourself. It is time, therefore, to develop a profile of your own patterns of thinking, behaving, and relating to others. It will be the combination of this profile data, that will enable you to make a well-informed decision based upon the critical factors that are important to your personal success (that is, your predictive model).

In this, and the following sections, you will be guided through a series of exercises that will help you learn important things about yourself. Certain of these things you will already understand, others will come into clearer focus, and a few will be completely new discoveries.

As a supplement to these exercises, you are encouraged to make use of an additional resource. David Kiersey and Marilyn Bates' book, *Please Understand Me* (Promethean Books, 1978) provides a comprehensive and easily understood explanation of personality types, career choice, relationship patterns, and thinking styles based upon the widely used and highly respected

Myers-Briggs Type Indicator (MBTI). A particularly helpful part of this book is a version of MBTI that you can complete and score on your own prior to reading the rest of the book.

DEVELOPING YOUR PERSONAL "CRITICAL 3" PROFILE

You will want to start this process by taking three clean sheets of white paper. Label each sheet in accordance with the three core job parts of the Critical 3 (i.e., Task Management, Self-Management, and Interpersonal Relationship Management). As you complete each of the following exercises, you will want to record the resulting list of words on the appropriate paper that corresponds to the area being probed.

As you complete the following exercises, it is important to remember that there aren't any "right" or "wrong" answers. As you read down the pairings in each list, therefore, simply choose the first word or phrase that "jumps out" as your preference. Don't over analyze or evaluate. It would be wise to adhere to that old adage—"To thine own self be true." These exercises are intended to help you, not anyone else. So, you will want to be candid and honest in your responses, being certain that you end up with an accurate profile that will help you to make an informed and intelligent employment decision.

Job Task—Trait Preferences

(Note: Record your choices on the Task Management Sheet (see example on Figure 1, p. 32) under the subheading "Job Trait Preferences.")

- Prefer to work with information _or_ hands-on problem-solving _or_ helping people.

- Prefer analyzing data _or_ using my instincts to make decisions.

- Prefer working with detail _or_ general trends.

- Prefer dealing with today's challenge _or_ long-term issues.

- Prefer complex tasks _or_ simplified ones.

- Prefer predictable work _or_ work that is full of surprises.

- Prefer to rely on procedure and precedent _or_ to break new ground.

- Prefer to maintain tradition _or_ to implement change.

- Prefer to improve what is _or_ to search for new opportunities.

- Prefer to play a supporting role _or_ to be at the point of action.

Self-Management — Trait Preferences

(Note: Record preferred choices on the Self-Management Sheet (see example on Figure 2, p. 33) under the heading "Self-Management—Trait Preferences.")

- Prefer to work in privacy _or_ to interact with others.

- Prefer to be able to plan out your day _or_ respond to a variety of unscheduled requests.

- Prefer to exercise independent judgment _or_ rely on policy and procedure when making decisions.

- Prefer to be an individual contributor _or_ a member of a team.

- Prefer personal recognition _or_ let the achievement be the recognition.

- Prefer to draw energy from my work _or_ relationships with those around you.

- Prefer to lead _or_ follow.

- Prefer to learn by doing _or_ from reading _or_ observing.

- Prefer to be known for your knowledge _or_ your interpersonal skills.

- Get it done yourself _or_ enable others to do it.

Interpersonal Trait Preferences

(Note: Record preferred choices on the Interpersonal Relationship Management Sheet (see example on Figure 3, p. 34) under the subheading "Interpersonal Trait Preferences.")

- Prefer to deal with conflict *or* keep the peace.

- Prefer to work with people one-on-one *or* in a group.

- Prefer to be actively involved in conflict resolution *or* let others work it out.

- Prefer to use authority *or* use negotiations to get action.

- Prefer to be seen as a boss *or* as a friend.

- While in a group, prefer to focus on the task *or* on the interaction between people.

- While in a group, would prefer to be the idea person *or* the director *or* the arbitrator.

- Prefer personal differences with others to be resolved *or* can live with the differences.

- Prefer to talk *or* to listen to others.

- Prefer initially to "connect" with others through ideas *or* through feelings.

Now that you have completed these exercises, take time to study the three trait preference lists that you have developed for some insight about yourself. Note, in particular, any recurring themes that appear on more than one of these lists. This will shed some light on your personal preferences for certain types of work and work environments that you find motivational. It will also provide you with an important part of the "predictive model," which should help you gauge the suitability of various employment opportunities throughout the course of your job search.

Take a moment, now, to look at the "sample" predictive model at the end of this chapter (see Figures 1, 2, & 3). Note how the information developed through the use of the last three exercises has been incorporated into the construction of the final predictive model design.

REFINING THE PREDICTIVE MODEL

Up to this point, we have been using William Crockett's concept of the Critical 3 as the basis for developing our predictive model. This approach, although excellent, has had a tendency to focus on the "present" and "future" dimensions of our job, self- and interpersonal trait preferences. An equally important dimension to consider in developing an effective job search plan and making an informed career decision, however, is our "past experience." These past experiences, in many ways, have helped to shape the way we are today, and offer a number of clues concerning our likes, dislikes, and preferences. They have the potential to provide us with a great deal of insight about what we enjoy and what motivates us.

In this section of the chapter, therefore, we will focus our attention on "past experience" to learn more about ourselves, and to provide the basis for further refinement of our personal predictive model. Specifically, we will be using the following exercises:

1. Motivational Mapping

2. Career Mapping

3. Best Boss Profiling.

As you complete each of the following exercises, you will want to review the data that has been generated, not only for its own value but also in the context of the partial predictive model profile that you have already developed. Where appropriate, you will want to add any new information that you discover about yourself and your preferences as a further refinement of your predictive model.

Motivational Mapping

In the following set of exercises, you will take a walk back through your past work experience to discover certain factors that have contributed to your level of job satisfaction/dissatisfaction (that is, your overall motivational level) throughout your working lifetime. When completing these exercises, you can think back on different types of jobs you have held—full-time, part-time, volunteer work—any work experience that you feel would be helpful to you in making your next career choice.

To prepare for this exercise, take a blank sheet of paper and draw a graph like the one shown in Figure 4 (p. 35). Depending on the length of your career to-date, you may want to use time intervals of either 1, 2, or 5 years on the horizontal axis to fit the width of your paper and at the same time reflect the full extent of your working years.

You will be completing this motivational map a total of three different times—plotting three separate factors (i.e., individual impact, team feeling, and sense of belonging) on the graph. Be sure, therefore, to use a different color for each of the three separate time-lines that you will plot. This color differentiation will make the graph much easier to read and interpret when you have finished plotting the three factors.

Use the 1 to 10 rating scale shown on the left (vertical) axis of the graph to indicate the level of satisfaction or dissatisfaction you felt for each job that you have held, and plot that rating directly above the year (see the horizontal time-line) in which that job was held by you.

When plotting the degree of job satisfaction/dissatisfaction experienced for each of your past positions, you will note that satisfaction ratings above the 0 level reflect an increasing level of satisfaction with the job, with the maximum rating of 10 representing the highest possible level of satisfaction. A rating of 0 reflects neither satisfaction nor dissatisfaction with a given job (i.e., a neutral feeling). By contrast, jobs rated below 0 reflect a level of increasing dissatisfaction, with a minus 10 rating representing "the pits" from a dissatisfaction standpoint.

For clarity and ease of interpretation, you may wish to briefly note the specific job title and company next to each job plotted on the graph. (See Figure 5, p. 36.)

Finally, before completing the next three mapping exercises, you may first want to spend a few moments studying the sample motivational map contained on page 36.

Individual Impact

The first line that you create on your motivational graph will be a line plot of your level of satisfaction/dissatisfaction for each of your past work experiences, based upon the degree of *individual impact* you felt that you had on the events around you while in that job. As you think about each past job experience you plot, therefore, you will want to consider such factors as your ability to exercise initiative, to be self-reliant, to make decisions, receive personal recognition for achievements, and to influence others to act.

Now, using these criteria, plot your level of satisfaction/ dissatisfaction for each position that you have held during your career lifetime. After plotting each of your past jobs with a point (or dot) on the graph, connect these dots with a red colored line. The resulting line plot should be labeled "Individual Impact." You may also wish to note job title and name of employer next to each of your plots to facilitate later interpretation of this graph.

Team Feeling

The second time-line that you will want to plot on your motivational map will be labeled "Team Feeling." This line will reflect the level of satisfaction/dissatisfaction you felt with each past work experience, based upon the degree to which you felt *part of a team effort*. Use the same rating process as before, label the resulting line plot "Team Feeling."

While completing this plot, think about such factors as the extent to which there was a cohesive team effort, the degree to which rewards reinforced team effort, how well people understood the big picture of the team's objectives, your personal sense of learning and achievement as a result of team cooperation.

Once you have plotted each of your past positions on this basis, it is suggested that you connect the resultant dots with a green line to distinguish it from "individual impact" line previously plotted.

You are now ready to plot the final line on your motivational graph.

Sense of Belonging

The third, and final, time-line to be plotted on your motivational map relates to sources of satisfaction/dissatisfaction that came from your sense of *belonging and fitting in.* This plot should be labeled "Sense of Belonging."

When plotting this line, think about the degree you felt you could be open with others, resolve conflict constructively, have your opinions listened to, and the degree to which people cared about each other.

Once you have plotted your level of satisfaction/dissatisfaction for each of your past positions, based upon your sense of belonging (i.e., fitting in), it is suggested that the resultant points be connected with a blue line to distinguish this from the previous two line plots (i.e., individual impact and team feeling).

Now that you have completed the motivational mapping exercise, scan all three of the time-lines that you have just plotted on the motivational map. Look for patterns or themes. Note, in particular, specific jobs that ranked unusually high or low in job satisfaction. Here are some guidelines and questions that should help you to make a proper analysis:

1. Note the relationship of the three line plots (i.e., personal impact, team feeling, and sense of belonging) to one another.

Which of the 3 appears to be most important to job satisfaction? Why?

Which of the 3 appears to be least important to job satisfaction? Why?

2. Which jobs rated highest overall in job satisfaction?

3. What specific factors accounted for your high level of satisfaction?

Job content?

Work environment?

Management style of your boss?

Intellectual challenge?

Freedom to act?

Etc., etc., etc.

Think hard about what was present (or absent) in both the job and the work environment that contributed to your overall job satisfaction. Be as specific as possible.

4. Which of your past positions ranked lowest in terms of level of job satisfaction? Why?

5. What specific factors most contributed to your dissatisfaction?

Job content?

Work environment?

Management style of your boss?

Freedom to act?

Etc., etc., etc.

Think hard about what was present (or absent) in both the job and work environment that accounted for your unhappiness. Be as specific as possible.

What have you learned from this mapping exercise? What new data do you now have that needs to be added to your predictive model that is not already there? Do any of your findings from this motivational mapping exercise modify (or refine) existing data contained in your predictive model? Utilize these findings to both add new data to your model and to modify and refine existing personal profile data as appropriate. Label this new information "Motivational Factors" and record the new data on the appropriate sheets (i.e., Task Management, Self-Management, Interpersonal Relationships Management) that comprise your predictive model. These changes should enhance the overall accuracy of your personal predicitve model, and provide you with the basis for making a more informed and intelligent job and career decision.

Career Mapping

We have just used past experience to plot an historical map of our past motivation and discover more about what motivates and/or demotivates us. We will now make use of "career mapping" as the basis for gaining some insight about the kind of work environments that have allowed us to be most productive (i.e., get the most out of us).

From this exercise, you will discover some additional things about yourself that should prove very helpful in determining the kind of work environment that you best fit.

For this exercise, think about your experiences in the overall work setting (i.e., job content, quality of work life, organizational culture, relationships with coworkers). As with motivational mapping, you are encouraged to draw on whatever work experiences you have had (e.g., part-time, full-time, volunteer activities) that will be helpful in gaining a clearer understanding of those organizational characteristics that are important to your personal job satisfaction and productivity.

For this exercise, take a sheet of paper and draw two vertical, parallel columns (see Figure 6). Label the left column "Best Aspects," and the right column "Worst Aspects." Next, take your mind back through each of your work experiences in your career to-date, including each job you have held in each organization you have been a part of. Use the chart that you have created to write down the 5 best and worst aspects of each of these positions. (Figure 6 on page 37 shows a completed career map.)

Having completed this exercise for all positions you have held, now scan down the columns you have created looking for common themes and patterns. Look particularly for recurring themes and the frequency with which they occur. Themes that are frequently repeated suggest that they have some relevance or importance to us beyond those themes that appear only once or twice.

By observing the frequency of occurrence, a pattern will likely emerge that can serve to provide you with a great deal of insight concerning those organizational factors that are important to personal satisfaction and successful performance. These should be compiled on a list entitled "Ideal Organizational Profile," and added to your profiles of the "Critical 3," as a part of your predictive model. (See Figure 7 on page 39 as an example.)

Profiling the "Best" Boss

The relationship with our boss is not only a critical factor in any job, it is also one of the most important role models we will have in our career. This is especially true when we find ourselves in a management role and seek a frame-of-reference to shape our own managerial style. How we have felt about a particular boss can provide some very helpful clues about those management traits and characteristics that are important to us for our personal success and happiness.

Take your time with this "best boss" profiling exercise if you wish to get maximum value from it. An effective relationship with a boss is more than just "good chemistry." It requires understanding, communication, knowing the work and thinking patterns of each other, how to sell ideas effectively, and how to most productively work through disagreements.

Start this exercise by first thinking about the various bosses that you have had in your career so far. If this is your first effort at seeking full-time employment, think about any bosses that you have had in part-time jobs and volunteer work, but also try to envision the kind of boss you would want to work for in that first job.

Now, having thought about these bosses, identify that one "best" boss—the one for whom you most enjoyed working—and complete the following exercise.

Profile of Best Boss

- Write a list of 10 phrases that best describe your best boss.

- What were the traits that made this person your best boss?

- Why are these traits important to you?

- How did these traits benefit you?

- How did you respond when these traits were exhibited by this boss?

- Why do you think you responded positively to them?

When responding to the above questions, think in terms of the "Critical 3." Think about how that best boss affected your work effort, the way in which you managed yourself, and how your interpersonal skills were affected. Record your answers on a sheet of paper labeled "Best Boss Profile," and add this sheet to your predictive model. (See Figure 8 on page 40 for an example of what a "Best Boss Profile" might look like.)

No boss is perfect, but it will be important for you to have a basis for evaluating future prospective bosses and predicting the impact they will have on you and your overall job and career satisfaction. The work may be exciting and stimulating, but if you and your boss are not compatible, life can become rather stressful and, sooner or later, you will likely be feeling pretty miserable.

Business Strategy and Individual Skills

The final consideration, in building your predictive model, is the determination of your fit with the overall business strategy of a prospective employer. If you do not have the skills and capabilities needed to support the business plans and strategies of a potential employer, you could be in for a short career.

The key question becomes, "With which type of business strategies are your skills most compatible?" The converse question is just as important to a solid employment marriage. "With which type of business strategies are your skills least compatible?"

Fortunately for job seekers, there is a great deal of information available about the relationship between business strategy and the skills individuals need in order to perform successfully in given strategic environments.

One of the best studies, which summarizes the linkage between business strategy and individual skills, is provided by Marc Gerstein and Heather Reisman. In this study, "Strategic Selection: Matching Executives to Business Conditions," published in the Winter 1983 issue of the *Sloan Management Review*, they provide a clear, concise description of this important linkage. Since this publication, experience has shown that the skills they identified are important, not just for executives, but for all levels of managements, and (to a lesser degree) nonmanagerial employees as well.

The following is a summary of those individual skills that are known to be most important for seven different business strategies. By reviewing the skills required by each of these seven business strategies with your own skills profile, you will be able to identify the type of strategic environments in which you will best function. Such review should also serve to point out those strategic environments in which you will be least effective, and which you should consciously avoid as part of your overall job hunting strategy.

There would certainly be no point for you to select an organization where your specific skills do not prepare you to perform well. Conversely, there would be every reason to search out those organizations where your skill base is compatible with (and supportive of) the company's primary strategic initiative.

Once you have identified the skill set(s) that most closely resemble(s) your own skills profile, list both the strategy and key skills profile on a separate sheet of paper entitled "Strategic Fit" and include this as part of your "predictive model." (See Figure 9, p. 41.)

Summary: Business Strategy & Key Skills

1. *START-UP*
   Create a vision of the business; establish core technical and marketing expertise; build a management team.
   Key Skills:
   - visionary
   - hands-on, action oriented
   - in-depth knowledge of area of responsibility
   - organization skills
   - staffing & selection skills
   - team builder
   - high energy

2. *TURNAROUND*
   Quick and accurate problem diagnosis; fix short-term problems; get control of the business
   Key Skills:
   - take charge orientation
   - analytical & diagnostic skills

- business strategist
- high energy
- risk taker
- can handle pressure
- good crisis manager
- negotiation skills

3. *EXTRACT PROFIT/RATIONALIZE*
Create stability; improve operating efficiencies; succession planning; anticipate change
   Key Skills:
   - knows the business
   - understands external dynamics
   - problem finder
   - administrative skills
   - systems thinker
   - builds relationships
   - able to identify employee potential & plan for their development
   - able to see opportunities for process improvement

4. *DYNAMIC GROWTH IN EXISTING BUSINESS*
Manage rapid change; increase market share, build for the long-term; develop a strategy
   Key Skills:
   - strategic & planning skills
   - visionary
   - able to manage priorities & contingencies
   - organizational skills
   - team builder
   - crisis management skills
   - moderate to high risk taker

- high energy
- staffing & selection skills

5. *REDEPLOYMENT OF RESOURCES*
Finding and optimizing core strengths; manage downsizing or restructuring
   Key Skills:
   - good political/social skills
   - persuasive
   - sensitive to negative impact on people
   - can selectively choose opportunities
   - good organizing skills
   - able to see the business holistically

6. *DIVESTING WEAK BUSINESSES*
Cutting losses; making tough decisions; knowing what to keep
   Key Skills:
   - willing to wear the black hat
   - tough minded
   - able to analyze cost vs. benefits
   - risk taker
   - doesn't need to be liked to feel good about self

7. NEW ACQUISITIONS
Integration of new units; optimize synergies; establish appropriate controls and communication processes
   Key Skills:
   - analytical abilities
   - relationship builder
   - able to build trust
   - good communicator
   - team builder

When reviewing this information, keep in mind that a department within a business may well be at a different point on the above continuum than the business itself. For example, you could be involved in the start-up of a new department as a result of high growth in a business. When this is the case, both sets of key skills (i.e., those for "start-up" business strategies and those for "dynamic growth" business strategies) become important. This is especially true if you will be in a management position in the firm.

You now have one final measurement tool to complete construction of your predictive model.

WHERE ARE WE?

You have just finished putting into place the most important building block of your job hunting campaign—your "predictive model." It is this model that can make the difference between simply "finding a job" and finding "job satisfaction and career happiness."

It is the latter that should be the "real goal" of any worthwhile job search effort. Anything short of this worthy objective will represent only a partial attainment of what we are all looking for in life (satisfaction and happiness), and a short time from now (measured in a few short months or a year or two) frustration will force us to once again enter the job market in search of those goals that are truly important to the quality and value of our lives.

At this point, we have developed a "Predicitve Model" comprised of the following components:

I. A Personal *Profile of the "Critical 3"*—Defining Your Optimal Job and Organizational Fit in 3 Critical Dimensions:

   A. Job Task Profile

   B. Self-Management Profile

   C. Interpersonal Relationships Management Profile

II. A Personal *"Motivational Mapping" Profile*—Using Past Work Experience to Define The Type of Organizational Culture Important to Your Personal Motivation, Job Satisfaction and Productivity (As Measured in 3 Dimensions):

   A. Your Individual Impact

   B. Your Feeling Part of a Team Effort

   C. Your Feelings of "Belonging" & "Fitting In"

III. A Personal *"Career Map" Profile*—Using Past Work Experience to Define Key Organizational Characteristics That Are Important to Your Personal Job Satisfaction and Productivity

IV. A *"Best Boss" Profile*—Using Your Best Boss to Define Those Traits and Characteristics That Are Important in a Boss in Order for You to Achieve a High Level of Job and Career Satisfaction

V. A *"Business Strategy" Profile*—Which Describes the Business Strategy(ies) for Which Your Core Skills are an Optimal Match

This combination of profiles, which comprises your "predictive model," puts you in a powerful position to measure and evaluate a host of employment opportunities and to "predict," with a high degree of objectivity and accuracy, the probability for a successful marriage. It serves as a measuring stick and constant reminder of those factors that are truly critical to your personal success and happiness.

In future chapters (especially those on interviewing and choosing the right employer), you will learn how to effectively use this predictive model to make an intelligent employment decision. In the meantime, you have put in place a critical component of your job hunting strategy that will become the focal point of much of your search process.

Sample
Predictive
Model

Figure 1   Task Management

Job Trait Preferences:

Prefer—To work with hands-on problem solving
—Using instincts to make decisions
—Working with general trends
—Dealing with today's challenges
—Complex tasks
—Work that is full of surprises
—To break new ground
—To implement change
—To search for new opportunities
—To be at the point of action

Motivational Factors (from Motivational Map):

Am Motivated by—Work offering variety of problems
—Work that has practical/tangible value
—Opportunity for major business impact
—Freedom to make decisions & act
—Work that requires creative thinking
—Position as key decision-maker
—Opportunity for broad strategic involvement
—Directing and motivating others

Figure 2   Self-Management

Self-Management—Trait Preferences:

Prefer—To work with others
— To respond to a variety of requests
— To exercise independent judgement
— To be a member of a team
— To let the achievement be the recognition
— To draw energy from relationships of those around me
— To lead
— To learn from doing
— To be known for interpersonal skills
— To enable others to do it

Motivational Factors (from Motivational Map):

Am Motivated by—Opportunity to operate under broad direction
— A boss who encourages reasonable risk-taking
— High performance expectations (quality)
— Freedom to make own decisions
— Broad strategic goals vs. detailed plans
— Opportunity to be key decision-maker
— Recognition for results/accomplishments
— Being part of key management team

Figure 3   *Interpersonal Relationship Management*

Interpersonal Relationship—Trait Preferences:

    Prefer—To deal with conflict
            —To work with people in a group
            —To be actively involved in conflict resolution
            —To use negotiations to get action
            —To be seen as a friend
            —To focus on interaction between people
            —To be the director
            —To resolve personal differences with others
            —To talk
            —To initially "connect" with others through ideas

Motivational Factors (from Motivational Map):

Am Motivated by—Working in a team environment
            —Open environment encouraging new ideas
            —Commitment to high quality & professionalism
            —Results focused vs. politically focused
            —Organization that values people vs. things
            —Boss who sees role as coach/teacher
            —A non-political culture
            —High performance expectations (broad goals)

Figure 4   *Motivational Map*

Level of Satisfaction

10

9

8

7

6

5

4

3

2

1

0—I—I—I—I—I—I—I—I—I—I—I—I—I—I—I—I—I—Today

Year

1

2

3

4

5

6

7

8

9

10

Level of Dissatisfacton

——————— = Individual Impact

------- = Team Feeling

〜〜〜〜〜 = Sense of Belonging

Figure 5   *Completed Motivational Map*

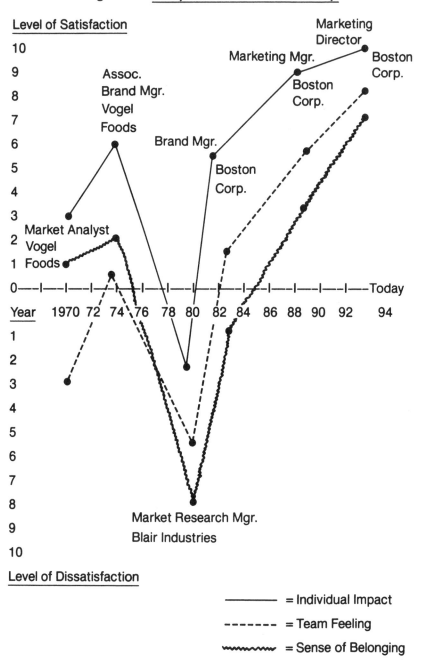

Level of Satisfaction

Marketing Director

Marketing Mgr.

Boston Corp.

Assoc. Brand Mgr. Vogel Foods

Boston Corp.

Brand Mgr.

Boston Corp.

Market Analyst Vogel Foods

Year   1970 72 74 76 78 80 82 84 86 88 90 92   94   Today

Market Research Mgr. Blair Industries

Level of Dissatisfaction

——————— = Individual Impact

------- = Team Feeling

wwwwww = Sense of Belonging

Figure 6   Career Map

Job/Company	Best Aspects	Worst Aspects
Market Analyst Vogel Foods	– Designing test markets – Good consumer marketing exposure	– Detailed number crunching – Narrow analytical focus – Little opportunity for creativity – Close supervision – Little meaningful impact – Boss took all the credit
Associate Brand Mgr. Vogel Foods	– Broader business exposure – Interface with other bus. disciplines	– Support vs. lead position – Follow other's ideas vs. own – Little opportunity for creative input
Market Research Mgr. Blair Industries	– Management of others – Leading, motivating others	– Highly political environment – Little sense of belonging – Data vs. people oriented job – Little creative opportunity – Boss liked to "micro-manage" – Indirect vs. direct business impact
Brand Manager Boston Corp.	– Good team environment – Tangible, measurable results – Freedom to make decisions – Management focus on results vs. process (i.e., how to)	– Narrow, single product focus – Desire broader business involvement

Figure 6   (Continued)

Job/Company	Best Aspects	Worst Aspects
Marketing Manager Boston Corp.	– Key member of business team – Highly visible, major impact – Freedom to make decisions – Leading, motivating others – Opportunity to use creativity – Good team environment	– Not directing total function – Desire more involvement (bus. strategy) – Some political decision-making
Marketing Director Boston Corp.	– Autonomy – Broad strategic involvement – Major, visible business impact – Key member of top mgt. team – Direct total function – Receive broad direction only – Intellectual, open culture – Emphasis on results vs. politics – Demanding, high performance expectations – Emphasis on quality & professionalism – Variety & challenge of problems	– Long hours – Little free time

Figure 7   *Ideal Organizational Profile*

—Encourages & rewards team efforts & results
—Non-political (focus is on results vs. personal connections)
—Top management provides broad direction only
—Top management doesn't "micro-manage" the business
—Provides opportunity for broad strategic involvement
—Provides freedom to act
—Values creativity & new ideas
—Values high quality & pursues continuous improvement
—Demanding (i.e., insists on performance excellence)
—Values knowledge & professionalism but rewards results
—Provides variety of problems & challenges
—Believes in involving its employees in decisions
—Values honesty & high integrity
—Strong competitive spirit (driven to be the leader)
—High morale (pride & strong team spirit)
—Provides opportunity to be part of top management group

Figure 8   "Best Boss" Profile

Best Boss—Descriptive Phrases/Traits:

- —Well-organized, systematic, logical
- —Demanding but fair
- —High expectations & performance standards
- —Non-political
- —Excellent teacher & coach
- —Strives for continuous improvement
- —Encourages subordinates to stretch & reach full potential
- —Open, honest, high integrity
- —Supportive—will fight for rights of subordinates
- —Provides broad direction with plenty of freedom to act
- —Good delegator

Importance of Traits to Me:

- —Set good role model
- —Forced me to grow & stretch personally & professionally
- —Built strong work ethic & appreciation for excellence
- —Built self-confidence & self-reliance

How I Responded & Why:

- —Worked hard & long hours
- —Sought to achieve high level of quality performance
- —Why?—We shared similar values & beliefs
    - —High level of personal & professional respect
    - —Strong desire to please & be recognized for superior contributions

Figure 9   Strategic Fit

Start-Up:

Create a vision of the business; establish core technical and marketing expertise; build a management team

   Key Skills:
   —Visionary
   —Hands-on, action oriented
   —Indepth knowledge of area of responsibility
   —Organization skills
   —Staffing & selection skills
   —Team building
   —High energy

Dynamic Growth in Existing Business:

Manage rapid change; increase market share; build for the long-term; develop a strategy

   Key Skills:
   —Strategic & planning skills
   —Visionary
   —Able to manage priorities & contingencies
   —Organizational skills
   —Team builder
   —Crisis management skills
   —Moderate to high risk-taker
   —High energy
   —Staffing & selection skills

3

Defining Your Job Objective

We have just completed the task of constructing your personal "predictive model," which will serve many purposes in helping you to formulate and execute an efficient and successful job hunting campaign. The main purpose of this predictive model, however, is to provide you with the basis for evaluating prospective employment opportunities and predicting the potential for a successful match.

This chapter is concerned with defining your job objective (that is, your functional job objective—the functional job that you are targeting for purposes of your job hunting campaign). The purpose of the job objective, unlike the predictive model, is not to provide the basis for evaluation of job opportunities. Instead, the role of the job objective is to provide a "point of focus" for both writing your resume and planning your job search process.

The job search process is far more efficient when it is structured around a well-defined job objective. Unless the job target or objective is clearly defined, the job hunting process stands little chance of success. Job searchers with vague objectives will spend much of their time aimlessly drifting like rudderless ships in the ocean. They will be at the mercy of the winds and tides, with little or no control over their final destination. There is no telling on what strange land they may run aground or how long they will continue to drift.

For a job hunting campaign to work, there must be a plan. For this plan to work, there must be a goal. All job hunting resources and strategies must be properly focused to maximize the probability for success. The goal provides the basis for such focus and, as such, is absolutely critical to the efficiency and overall success of the job search plan.

CAREER TESTING SERVICES

If you are just starting your career and are in a quandry about what to do with your life, I strongly recommend use of a good career testing and counseling service. You will find this to be money well spent.

Because there are several private firms that provide this type of consulting service, it may be difficult to distinguish between the professionals and the charlatans. I would recommend that you look into the career testing and counseling services provided by reputable universities. Many of these offer services to not only the student body but the general public as well. Fees may vary substantially, but you should be able to get this kind of assistance for somewhere in the $150 to $500 range.

Most of these university programs offer a day or two of intense testing followed by individual counseling. Tests normally examine IQ, personality, aptitude, and interest. This program is usually housed in the university's psychology department, and counselors are advanced degreed psychologists with specific training in career counseling.

One customary result of these tests is a comparison of your personal traits, interests and aptitudes with those who are successfully employed in a wide range of occupations. By making these comparisons, the psychologist is able to suggest various occupations that appear to be particularly suited to your specific profile. Conversely, you are counseled to avoid certain occupations that do not appear suitable, based upon this profile comparison method.

These career testing and counseling programs are usually quite effectual in helping one narrow down the choices. Following such counseling, a little practical research, including visitations with persons now employed in the recommended occupations, can usually narrow the field considerably more and allow you to select a career objective.

ELEMENTS OF SUCCESSFUL GOAL SETTING

The elements of successful job goal setting are as follows:

1. Goals must be realistic.

2. Goals must be achievable.

3. Goals must be well-defined.

If any of these elements is missing, there is a good possibility that the entire job search process will flounder and eventually fail. Let's examine each of these elements in greater detail.

Realistic

It is important, when establishing your job goal, that this goal be realistic. It would be unrealistic for someone with only two years of experience, to think that he or she could land a job at the vice-presidential level. It would be equally outrageous to think that someone without a degree in chemistry could work as a research chemist in a major company. These are unreasonable goals and, as such, are likely not achievable.

If you are interested in a certain career area and are uncertain whether you are being realistic in your expectations, I would suggest that you seek the practical advice of someone who is already employed in such a position. Or, you might consider discussing the matter with a seasoned employment professional who has hired numerous people into your targeted position.

With appropriate advice from knowledgeable sources, you may find that you need to readjust your sights to a lower and more fitting position.

Achievable

There are many who would like to be President of the United States. Simply wanting to be President doesn't mean that this is an achievable objective. *Desire alone is not enough* to accomplish your goals; you must also have the necessary skills and experience to make achievement possible. If your job objective is to be attainable, your qualifications must be sufficient enough to warrant serious consideration. Without these prerequisites, your job search will most certainly end in frustration.

Here again, it is important for you to seek some knowledgeable advice, should you have questions concerning the accessibility of your desired career. It is best to seek such advice from persons already employed in such capacity or from those who frequently are involved in hiring persons for such positions.

Well-Defined

It is not enough for a job objective to be realistic and achievable; it must also be well-defined. It is difficult to build a meaningful job search strategy if your job objective is too obscure. For the most desirable results, your job objective should be specific in the following dimensions:

1. Organizational level

2. Functional area

3. Specialty (if required)

4. Industry

5. Geography

Using these parameters, a proper statement of objective would be:

> I seek a position as Director of Corporate Accounting in the banking or financial management field located in the northeastern United States.

This is a well-defined objective that will allow you to maximize the job search planning process and focus your job search resources for optimal results.

In contrast, consider this poorly defined objective:

> I seek a director level position in the financial field.

As you can readily see, it will be much more difficult to put together a meaningful job search strategy to meet this objective than in the preceding example. Without definition of the functional specialty and geographical zone, the job objective is so vague that a meaningful job search plan becomes very difficult to draft.

It should also be pointed out that the lack of a well-defined objective will also impair the preparation of a good resume. A resume based on a vague objective can not be properly tailored to showcase your relevant skills, capabilities and experience. Likewise, it will make it harder to plan a decent interview strategy.

Overall, a poorly defined job objective will substantially reduce the effectiveness of your entire job search campaign.

ESTABLISHING YOUR JOB OBJECTIVE

Using the advice and guidelines provided in this chapter, try writing your own statement of job hunting objective by completing the following statement:

I seek a position as _____ in the _____ field located in _____.

Now test whether this objective is realistic and achievable by asking yourself the following questions:

1. Does my current job level support the job level that I am seeking?

2. Does my level of experience support the job level that I am seeking?

3. Do my qualifications (education, knowledge, skills, experience) support the functional area and specialty that I am seeking?

4. Will I be able to successfully compete with other qualified persons competing for this position?

5. Is my job objective both realistic and achievable?

If you have been able to answer each of these questions in the affirmative, you have formed a realistic, achievable, and well-defined job objective around which to structure a job search campaign. Having established this job objective, your next step in the job search process is employment resume preparation. The next few chapters will deal with the subject of resume selection and preparation, a very important part of the job hunting process.

4

The Difference:
Good vs. Bad Resumes

Writing an effective resume is no accident. It doesn't just happen. One cannot expect to sit down the night before that all-important interview and write a resume that will amply represent his or her background, including education, knowledge, skills, and relevant experience. Such crash attempts usually fall miserably short of the mark and, instead of creating a favorable impression, serve to scuttle the interview even before it gets started.

Resume writing requires careful thought and planning. As a vital part of your job search, it is a task that deserves your maximum effort.

RESUME PURPOSE

What is the role of the resume in the employment process? How is it used and by whom?

Knowing the answer to these, and similar questions, is paramount to a well-formulated resume. It is important to design a resume that will meet the needs of the interviewer/employer—one that is easily read and focuses on those items cogent to the employer's evaluation and selection process.

Before proceeding with the resume preparation process, it is important to have a thorough understanding of what this document is intended to accomplish. Unfortunately, many employment candidates have a somewhat narrow understanding of the role of the resume, and therefore, end up with something that is inappropriate, at best.

The primary purpose of the resume is to serve as a tool in helping you secure an employment interview. It must therefore convince a prospective employer that you are an outstanding candidate, who has something of value to contribute to the organization, and that it will be well worth his or her time to grant you a personal interview. The key word here is *value.* The resume must convey that somehow the company's performance and profitability will be enhanced by hiring you.

Therefore, the resume should emphasize your major contributions and accomplishments. It must not simply state the names of past employers and list the job titles of past positions that you have held. These factors alone cannot be expected to convince an employer of your merit. Instead, your resume must convince the employer that you are someone who will bring improvements and make worthwhile contributions through the solution of major problems and issues confronting the organization. Only past accomplishments will serve *to make the sale.*

Although the primary function of the resume is to help you to secure an employment interview, it also serves two important additional purposes as well:

1. First, it serves as a road map for your employment interview. In most cases, the interviewer will use it as an outline to guide the discussion, and to focus on those aspects of your qualifications that you have chosen to highlight.

2. Second, after the interview has taken place and you have departed, the interviewer will use the resume as a reference source for recalling and/or further evaluating your specific strengths and abilities, as well as comparing them to others who are being considered for the position.

Keeping in mind these functions, it is easy to understand just how critical the resume is to the outcome of the employment process. It should also be evident to you that, while preparing this important document, you will need to pay particular attention to its sales appeal. If it is to convince a prospective employer to interview and hire you, it must present your qualifications in the most favorable light, focusing on past accomplishments and results. Additionally, it must continue to remind the prospective employer of your excellent qualifications and value long after the interview discussion has been concluded.

CHARACTERISTICS OF POOR RESUMES

What are the differences between a good resume and a bad resume? By being aware of these distinctions, you will be better prepared to critique your own resume and avoid the common pitfalls of bad resume preparation.

What are the characteristics of poor resumes? Here are some that commonly account for resume ineffectiveness:

1. Poor Organization—difficult to read (see Resume A)

2. Sloppiness—conveys carelessness (see Resume B)

3. Narrative Approach—too much time to read (see Resume C)

4. Job Function vs. Accomplishments Focus—fails to sell capability (see Resume D)

5. Insufficient Information—can't fully evaluate (see Resume E)

6. Too Much Information—too much time to read (see Resume F)

7. Puffery and Bragging—insults employer's intelligence (see Resume G)

Let's now examine these characteristics more closely so that you can clearly see their disadvantages.

Poor Organization

Resume A on the next page is an example of poor organization. Visual examination alone shows the following disadvantages:

1. Is difficult to read

2. Takes too much time to read

3. Key information difficult to locate

4. Suggests writer is disorganized and does not think clearly

This kind of resume does little to improve your chances of landing a job interview, let alone providing the foundation for a successful one. You can be sure, with such a poor resume, that the employer will be compelled to use much of your valuable interview time simply trying to ferret out basic information about your background. Little interview time will likely be left to explore your unique skills and value. A poorly organized resume therefore, puts you at a distinct disadvantage as it devitalizes your interview.

As you can see, a little organization can go a long way to improving your employment chances. Take time to develop a well-organized resume.

Resume A—Poor Organization

Investment Banker with 17 year record of success in Mergers, Acquisitions, Joint Ventures and Capital Formation now seeking to apply skills in corporate situation. International experience, multi-lingual, U.S. citizen. Young, articulate, presents self well. Pleasant, friendly, people-oriented.

David K. Larson

H: 512/337-9872   325 Pierson Street
W: 512/887-9823   Detroit, MI 22398

Current Responsibilities

Relocating to Atlanta in 1983, I established an independent consulting practice making use of my skills in:

—Business Development	—Valuations
—Transaction analysis	—Negotiations
—Industry search	—Debt and equity financing

My successes here (since 1983) include:

- Major transactions and new development of hotels in Atlanta, Tampa, Mobile, New Orleans and Miami.
- Expansion of sewer service through industrial revenue development bonds.
- Refinancing development of waste disposal facilities through I.D.R. bonds.

Earlier Accomplishments

As Vice President Zebco Enterprises on the West Coast (1978–1983):

—Successfully invested $2.5 million in several real estate development transactions, some with debt to equity ratio of 25 to 1.

- Sell-outs averaged up to 200% return for investors.

As Vice President of Consolidated Enterprises in Boston (1974–78):

—Successfully accomplished leveraged buy-out of a candy manufacturer, flour blending plant, four hotels, two land parcels, manufacturer of frozen pastries as well as several homes

- All purchases proved profitable
(up to 200% return) for investors.

Resume A —(Continued)

From 1970–74, I managed investments in Kenya for an investor group seeking Black nationals to buy businesses owned by whites seeking to leave Africa.

—Secured 100% financing for buyer's group for three major companies

- Providing sellers cash purchase at full asking price.

Assigned management responsibilities for conglomerate (tour operators, hardware store, auto imports, finance company and service stations)

Added four new companies. Increased unit sales 12% and tripled corporate profitability.

Personal Background

Studying under the Cambridge University program while living in England, I completed a degree in Mathematics and, in 1970, finished first out of 18,000 taking tests for accreditation by the Association of Certified and Corporate Accountants. (C.P.A. equivalency) Only 18% passed the examination.

Continuing education includes ongoing program or related conferences and workshops. Regularly read a wide range of business and news publications.

Age 39, divorced, no dependents. Free to travel extensively.

Detailed references furnished upon request.

Sloppiness

Resume B is an example of sloppiness. In addition to a smudge mark and a coffee stain on the paper itself, the resume is also poorly prepared. There are several spelling errors, missing words, irregular margins, inconsistent underlining of key sections, manual corrections, manual underlining, and so on. Most employers, receiving a resume in this condition, would simply not even bother to read it.

Among the many disadvantages of a sloppy resume are:

1. Creates poor impression with employer

2. Is difficult to read

3. Detracts from content

4. Suggests writer is careless, irresponsible, and lacks personal pride

5. Suggests writer is prone to error, is inaccurate, and lacks thoroughness

6. Suggests writer lacks initiative and motivation

There is really no excuse for a sloppy resume. If you are poor at spelling or grammar, seek the assistance of someone who is strong in these areas. Have your resume proofread and make necessary corrections before it goes to press. Likewise, if you are a poor typist, take your resume to a professional typist and have it done right.

Your resume is usually the very first contact that an employer has with you. It is important, therefore, that it represents you as someone who is neat, thorough, accurate, organized, responsible, and well-motivated. A sloppy resume creates the opposite impression and serves as a very real barrier to a successful employment campaign.

Resume B —Sloppiness

Richard R. Johnson
325 East Exton Stree
Richboro, Pennsylvannia 8872

Phone: (313) 675-2371

<u>Objective</u>: To find a responsible posiition in Operations Management
with a major manufacturing compan∳y.

<u>Education</u>: B.S. Degree, Industrial Engineering
University of Virginia, 1978

<u>Work Experience</u>:

1980–1987 <u>Manufacturing Manager,</u> Rammar Corporation,
Philadelphia, Pennsylvannia.:
      I report to the Derector of Manufacturing and managed a
      150 employee department engaged in the manufacture of
printed circuit boards for computer-controlled drill presses. In the last
3 years have incresed output by 35% and reduced manufacturing
      costs by 18%, at the same time reducing employee
headcount by 5%. Operating budget is $35 Million with value of goods
      manufacturied in the $62 range.
             ^Million

1978–1980 <u>Shift Supervisor,</u> Duncan Corporation, Lansdale, PA.
      Worked two yeras as the Shift Supervisor for
the ——→Rotor Division. Managed group of 27 hourly workers in the
    manufacture of stainless steel rotors for adverse environment
motors.

<u>Hobbies</u>: Reading, running, sailing, fishing and card playing.

  <u>Professional Affiliations</u>:
      Member—Philadelphia Area Engineers' Club-1979 to present.
      Member—Industrial Engineering Assoc.—1980 to 1986

<u>Personal</u>:
    Age   : 30
    Height   : 5'10"
    Weight   : 175 pounds
    Marital Status: Single (Engaged)

Straight Narrative Approach

Resume C is an example of the straight narrative approach. As you can see, this style reads very much like a letter and sets forth the candidate's background in paragraph form.

Although at first glance, this resume may seem quite acceptable to the inexperienced job seeker, I can assure you that seasoned employment professionals do not share this feeling. For the person who must read your resume and decide whether you warrant further consideration, there are several drawbacks to this type of resume. They are as follows:

1. Takes too much time to read

2. Forces employer to read entire resume in order to get key information (many won't bother)

3. Suggests writer does not have sufficient motivation or patience to write proper resume

4. Suggests writer may be naive about proper resume format and acceptable business protocol

5. Suggests writer may also be ignorant about other acceptable business practices and courtesies

6. Suggests the writer simply doesn't care.

The job seeker places himself/herself at a real disadvantage when utilizing the straight narrative form of resume. Using a proper resume format will, in most cases, contribute to the success of your job search. Take the time to research and utilize an acceptable resume format, rather than simply using the straight narrative approach. This could spell the difference between a fruitful campaign and one that ends in failure.

Resume C —Straight Narrative Approach

JOHN R. SMITH
1324 Donovan Terrace
Rockville, MD 97218

Phone: Office—(312) 893-1724
Home—(312) 892-1754

I am a chemical engineer with an M.B.A. and have 20 years of experience to bring to a future employer.

Joining my current employer, Ace Chemical Corporation, a Fortune 100 firm, in 1967, I held operations management positions of increasing responsibility for ten years, including one year of insurance and development. In my most recent operations and engineering management positions, I supervised hourly and salaried personnel in production, maintenance, and shipping. I was also responsible for overseeing the environmental and water treatment functions for pH control in the production of caustic soda.

Earlier, I served as General Foreman in polymer production, where I supervised production operations, maintenance, shipping, and quality control including inventory of finished product, production equipment, and sales requirements. Prior to this, as Senior Operations Engineer, I was responsible for diverse technical projects for the improvement of production rates and quality, increased yields, reduction of operations and maintenance expenses, manpower reduction requirements, and supervision and training of equipment operators.

Previously, as Process Engineer, I served as liaison between production and R & D to resolve critical problems in the nylon product lines. This included preparing various economic studies on alternatives, plus bench scale and pilot scale studies, and full scale plant experiments of special operating parameters. As Operations Engineer, I supervised a staff of 85 equipment operators in the raw materials and unloading section, and performed analytical testing and studies in quality control and operating rates.

Resume C —(Continued)

My recent experience, since 1979, in Product Management and Regional Sales and Marketing has encompassed significant responsibility. As Regional Manager, I achieved personal annual sales of $92 million to major accounts and, as Area Sales Manager, I was responsible for territories with annual sales up to $139 million. I developed sales and marketing strategies for several chemical products and managed a sales and clerical support staff in a 22 state region.

Personally, I am 45 years of age, married, have six children; and earned by M.B.A. degree from the University of Maryland, and my Chemical Engineering degree from Drexel University in Philadelphia. My present salary is $85,000 per year.

Job Function vs. Accomplishments Focus

Resume D focuses on job function rather than on the individual's accomplishments. Reading this is like reading a job description rather than a resume. As you read it, you get the feeling that the resume is more an account of the positions performed than it is a portrayal of the person who has performed them. Such a resume is boring. Other adjectives which also come to mind are bland and inanimate. It does little to create any enthusiasm or excitement about the candidate and his/her capabilities.

Major disadvantages of this kind of resume are:

1. Fails to sell candidate's capability

2. Focuses on functions performed rather than results achieved

3. Makes boring reading

Admittedly, this is not an altogether bad approach to resume writing. It does at least list each position held along with an explanation of the functional responsibilities for which the candidate has been accountable. This does provide some basis for proper evaluation of the candidate.

The point is, however, that the resume can be improved by adding some of the major accomplishments realized while the candidate was in these positions. The inference that is drawn by employers from such inclusion is that the candidate is well-motivated and results-oriented. This is in contrast with the person who is satisfied with the status quo and who will simply perform the job as it has always been performed. Instead, most companies would much prefer to hire persons who will make changes, bring improvement, and add value to the organization. Statements of results achieved, along with a description of functional responsibilities, clearly play an important role in developing a resume that will be effective.

Resume D—Job Function vs. Accomplishments Focus

CATHERINE F. GILES
816 Wacker Avenue
Detroit, MI 19875

Phone: (422) 897-1141

Education:

Ph.D., Industrial Psychology
University of Michigan, 1968

M.S., Industrial Relations
Michigan State University, 1966

B.A., Human Resource Management
Michigan State University, 1964
Summa Cum Laude

Professional Experience:

1970 to Present   Paxton Motor Corporation, Corporate Offices
East Lansing, Michigan

1986 to Present   Vice President—Human Resources: Report directly
to the President of this 2,500 employee, $500
million manufacturer of speciality motors. Manage
staff of 35 with functional responsibility for human
resource planning, organization design and
development, training, compensation and benefits,
and E.E.O.

1980–1986   Director Human Resources—Recco Division:
Reported to Vice President Human Resources—
Corporate Staff. Responsibilities included wage
and salary administration, organization design,
benefits administration, labor relations, training and
development, safety and hygiene, and medical.

Resume D —(Continued)

1975–1980	Personnel Manager—Kingston Plant: Reported to Plant Manager with indirect responsibility to the Director of Human Resources—Recco Division. Was accountable for all plant H.R. functions, including: wage and salary administration employee relations, labor negotiations, training and development, benefits, safety, hygiene and medical.
1970–1975	Consultant—Corporate Organization Effectiveness: Reported to the Director of Organization Development. Provided consulting support to both the Recco and Stevens Divisions in the areas of socio-technical system implementation, team building and participatory management techniques.
1968–1970	The Polaris Corporation, Overstad Division East Lansing, Michigan
	Consultant—Organization Design: Reported to the Corporate Director of Human Resources. Provided consulting support in the area of organization design and development.

Personal:

	Age	: 47
	Height	: 5′4″
	Weight	: 140 pounds
	Marital Status:	Divorced, 3 Children
	Health	: Excellent

Insufficient Information

Resume E is an example of insufficient information. Important data which most employers need for determining whether they have an interest in the candidate is missing. Use of such a resume places the job hunter at a disadvantage when compared to other well-qualified candidates who have been more disclosing.

Key information that is missing from this resume is as follows:

1. No statement of job objective

2. No statement of educational qualifications

3. No description of functional responsibilities for past positions held

4. No description of size and scope of positions held

5. No description of major results and accomplishments for each position previously held.

As an experienced employment professional, who has worked for better than 25 years as an executive search consultant and as a Fortune 200 human resources executive, I can tell you that the missing information cited here is what most seasoned employment professionals look for in a well constructed resume. It is key information that is important to making a preliminary determination of interest in the candidate.

It is important that both the right amount and right kind of information be presented in the resume if it is to serve you well in the interview process. Be careful, therefore, that your resume is not incomplete.

Resume E—Insufficient Information

Ann C. Johnson
824 Spruce Street
Denver, Colorado 87723

Phone: (315) 267-8759 (O)
(315) 267-8970 (H)

My MBA and early background in finance (CPA with strong commercial lending experience for a regional bank) enabled me to make the transition into general management easily. As a general manager, I have placed strong emphasis on sales/marketing, diversification of products, refinancing, and acquisitions/joint ventures. In summary, I have been the prime mover in corporate expansion and growth.

CAREER HIGHLIGHTS

- Increased sales by 75% in an industry where sales declined by 25%.

- Realized savings of $20,000 annually through installation and operation of new equipment and the negotiation of labor, purchasing, and financing contracts.

- Created unique loan packages and banking services, resulting in substantial return.

WORK HISTORY

Denver Bag Company
1981 to Present—Exec. V.P. & Gen. Manager
1979 to 1981—Controller/Treasurer

First National Bank of Georgia
1978 to 1979—Assist. V.P. Commercial Loans

First National Bank of Denver
1976 to 1978—Section Head/Credit Analysis

Too Much Information

Having too much information in your resume is as bad as, if not worse than, presenting the employer with insufficient information.

Resume F is an example of too much information. This approach places the job seeker at a very real disadvantage and should be avoided at all cost.

Notable problems with resumes of this sort are as follows:

1. Takes too much time to read

2. Key information not readily visible

3. Suggests writer lacks good judgment; lacks ability to separate the important from the unimportant

4. Suggests writer is unnecessarily verbose

5. Suggests writer may be naive about proper resume format and acceptable business protocol

6. Suggests writer may also be ignorant of other acceptable business practices and courtesies or, worse yet, doesn't care.

Each of the above is an excellent reason why the job hunter should avoid writing a resume that is too long. Presenting a proper balance of information (not too much and not too little) is very essential to resume effectiveness. Resumes that are either too long or too short can present a serious handicap to an otherwise productive job hunting campaign.

Resume F—Too Much Information

Allen B. Barber
226 Master Blvd.
Reading, PA 19886

Phone: (215) 875-9961

BSME, University of Pennsylvania, 1960
Pennsylvania Registration #55798
Member, National Society of Professional Engineers (NSPE)
Member, Society of Petroleum Engineers (SPE)
Member, American Society of Mechanical Engineers (ASME)

<u>Personal</u>: Currently employed with Scantia Technology. References will be furnished upon request. Credible work history maintained throughout career. Work generally obtained through personal acquaintances. Work never left unfinished or incomplete (except for companies discontinuing operations).

<u>Objective</u>: Work career and senior level of technical/administrative ability have endowed a combination of highly diversified skills and ready association with a broad perspective of most problems encountered, i.e. all prior assignments have varied considerably in scope. This has produced the ability to perform immediately with little (if any) learning curve. My objective is to obtain challenging employment in a growth market and to apply my above described credentials in continuation of a successful career. This objective represents an interest in either direct employment or as a consultant, and further includes an open mind to domestic or international relocation.

EXPERIENCE OVERVIEW:

<u>Excellent overall technical and administrative skills</u> founded upon twenty-seven years of involvement in numerous, diversified market environments including: mechanical designs, pneumatics/hydraulics, systems, testing, developmental, reliability/quality control, construction, analytical, manufacturing, management/administrative and marketing. Most recent specialty areas include equipment designs and systems engineering. Have been employed as an independent consultant for past six years.

Resume F —(Continued)

Market environments reflecting the above acquired skills include energy, aerospace, defense, utilities, and manufactured housing.

Titles include: Consultant, Manager of Engineering (3 positions), Project Manager, Project Engineer, Design/Senior Design Engineer, Reliability/Quality Control Engineer, Test Engineer/Supervisor, Market Research Analyst, Senior Staff Engineer, Manufacturing Engineer, Engineering Coordinator, Systems Engineer, Stress Analyst, Piping Designer and Draftsman.

Employer Affiliations include a wide range of blue chip companies, many of which reflect contract work and assignments in volatile, unstable job markets, i.e. aerospace, defense and energy. Firms for which I have worked include the following:

1987	Scantia Corporation	1972	Franklin Space Company
1986	Austin Latril	1971	Offshore Drilling Co.
1985	Houston Oil	1970	Tankland Corporation
1985	Tarracott Corp.	1969	California Energy Corp.
1984	Marshall Engineering	1968	Poe & Daggert Utilities
1983	Foster Wheeler Corp.	1967	Potter Engine Company
1982	Orvield Bach Co.	1966	General Electric Co.
1980	Carter Jet Engine Co.	1962	National Lead Company
1976	Ford Bacon Engineers	1960	Carson Instruments
1974	Eastman Kodak	1959	Litton Industries

EXPERIENCE DETAILS

Mechanical Designs: Prepared engineering, conceptual designs, layouts, details and bills of materials for numerous products including structural operating machinery, material handling and piping systems for hydroelectric and steam plants at TVA and Corps of Engineers. Also responsible for flight hardware test equipment for Saturn engines, instrument packages, launch support facilities, designs for pneumatic/hydraulic panels and equipment installations at NASA, Huntsville and the Cape. Involved in the design of flight systems payload experimental hardware and Astronaut crew systems equipment such as waste management, life support systems, extra vehicular space suit, safety equipment, utilities, bio-medical equipment and personal garments for duration of Apollo, Skylab, and briefly for

Resume F —(Continued)

the Shuttle programs. Heavy background in rotating equipment such as pumps, gas compressors, turbines, co-generation packages, valves, piping systems, skid-mounted packages, including all structural, instrumentation, piping equipment and materials selections. Provided process design of all oil and gas production equipment, engineered mechanical equipment for offshore drilling and production subsea, and on acoustic inspection device, subsea hydraulic control packages, Arctic drilling systems, subsea pumping, subsea process and new methods involving improved efficiencies/reliability. Designed commercial air conditioning system while overseas (Saudi Arabia).

SYSTEMS: Systems engineering, analysis and evaluations involving Astronaut crew systems interface with flight hardware; NASA payload systems reliability interface involving failure mode analysis for a variety of flight equipment, space hardware configuration control interface, NASA launch support systems facility interface; NASA/DOD hardware system milestone reviews with vendors. Engineered oil and gas package drilling and production systems for land and subsea, including controls, process, safety, maintenance and operations (there were numerous equipment subsystems, all of which functioned as a total system). Also, reviewed and checked drawings of complete assemblies/details.

TESTING: Supervised group responsible for environmental simulation testing of Apollo flight hardware at the Langston Flight Center, including failure analysis. Supervised testing of Skylab flight hardware used by Astronauts at Johnson Space Center. Engaged in testing of flight hardware on classified DOD project at Eastman Kodak. Responsible for systems testing (land and subsea) of hydraulic/pneumatic control packages and power packages. Responsible for rotating equipment and valve testing including failure, pressure, functional and systems. Responsible for numerous packaged systems customer acceptance tests.

RELIABILITY/QUALITY ASSURANCE: Responsible for vendor compliance with NASA reliability and quality assurance codes and standards for assigned flight hardware including medical experiments and crew equipment while with Carter Company. Prepared failure effects analysis (FMEA) and failure analysis.

Resume F —(Continued)

ANALYTICAL: Good analytical skills in a variety of fields spanning refrigeration and air conditioning, structural stress analysis, piping stress analysis, mechanical equipment designs and selections, power trains, pneumatics/hydraulics, computer applications and process designs.

MANUFACTURING: Numerous manufacturing environments including nuclear weapons production, valve and mechanical equipment manufacturing and manufacturing of packaged skid-mounted mechanical systems. Skills utilized included drawing compliance, quality assurance, reliability, machining operations, welding, tolerances, dimensional buildup, scheduling etc.

CONSTRUCTION: Served as construction site engineer with Carter steam plant in Pennsylvania, supervising mechanical equipments installations. Served as construction engineer for numerous oil and gas, mechanical and process packages from one to several hundred tons installed on platforms. Served as construction coordinator for waste water treatment plant in Philadelphia.

MARKETING: Heavy marketing skills throughout career. Wide variety of proposal management activities too numerous to describe, including technical writing and editing, heavy budgeting and estimating experience, and scheduling associated with proposals. Diverse markets such as search lights for helicopters, solar cells and solar astronomical instruments are included.

ADMINISTRATIVE: Manager of engineering departments for two major mechanical equipment manufacturers (approximately 60 people in each department) and a consultant company. Contracts administrator for aerospace equipment with NASA contractors; served on contract negotiating teams. Served in numerous project management positions with cost responsibility for engineering of up to $2 million, including purchasing, scheduling, clerical etc.

CODE FAMILIARITY: ASME, ANSI, MMS, API, NFPA, ASHRAE, AISC, ASTM. Experience also with MIL-STD, DOD and NASA standards.

Puffery and Bragging

A candidate's use of puffery or bragging can substantially detract from an otherwise acceptable resume. Resume G is an example of such.

Although it has often been said that the employment interview is the time to brag, to toot your own horn (and I generally agree), this is not true of the employment resume. The resume is intended to present a factual chronology of your background; it is not intended as a medium for extolling your many virtues. It is simply intended to present an honest account of where you've been and what you've accomplished.

To the experienced employment professional, attempts at self-evaluation in the resume document are usually seen as amateurish at best and, at worst, downright insulting. Seasoned professionals prefer to make their own evaluation of a candidate's strengths and weaknesses, and are sometimes resentful of an attempt to influence their judgment in what they consider to be a proprietary area which is their sole domain. Use of puffery and bragging in the resume compounds and intensifies these feelings.

Key disadvantages of using bragging or puffery in the resume are as follows:

1. Suggests writer is insensitive to professional role of interviewer

2. Suggests writer is unaware of proper business practice and acceptable protocol

3. Suggests writer considers interviewer naive

4. Wastes valuable space that could be better used to further describe functional responsibilities, job scope, and major accomplishments.

Although puffery or bragging should never be used, should you wish to delineate your major strengths, the cover letter that accompanies your resume is a far more appropriate place to accomplish this objective. Under no circumstances, however, use the resume to accomplish this.

Resume G—Puffery and Bragging

Linda B. Carver
421 South Warren Street
Chicago, IL 87326

Phone: (315) 473-9872

OBJECTIVE: Controller for major hospital or other health care institution.

MAJOR STRENGTHS:

- Adjust well to rapidly changing environments and circumstances.

- Professional...Responsible...Accurate...Thorough.

- A creative problem solver...analytical, decisive.

- Highly creative, innovative, resourceful.

- Very responsive to pressure and deadlines.

- Known for getting superior results and delivering highest quality work.

- Personable, exceptionally well-liked...get along with everybody.

- High energy, forceful, dynamic, results-oriented.

EDUCATION:

M.S., Accounting & Finance
University of Wisconsin, 1969

B.A., Business Administration
Western Michigan University, 1967

Resume G —(Continued)

EMPLOYMENT HISTORY:

1978–1987	Chicago Memorial Hospital, Chicago, IL
1982–1987	Hospital Administrator
1978–1982	Controller
1972–1978	Saint Francis Hospital, Naperville, IL
1974–1978	Assistant Controller
1972–1974	Senior Accountant
1969–1972	Keefer Nursing Home, Chicago, IL
	Accountant

PERSONAL:

Age	: 41
Height	: 6'2"
Weight	: 225 pounds
Marital Status:	Married, 3 Children
Health	: Excellent

CHARACTERISTICS OF GOOD RESUMES

We have now had a fairly thorough review of bad resumes, and I have shared a number of examples with you. But what about good resumes? What makes an employment resume effective?

It will probably come as little surprise that the characteristics of good resumes are the opposite of poor resumes. The good resume is carefully written to incorporate certain characteristics that, in themselves, assure that the final product will be both professional and meaningful.

Key characteristics of good resumes are:

1. Neat

2. Well-organized

3. Easily and quickly read

4. Key information highly visible

5. Proper length—not too long, not too short

6. Includes brief, but complete job descriptions

7. Depicts key accomplishments

8. Comprehensive—provides complete accounting of key areas of interest to prospective employers.

Resume H is an example of a good resume. You will note that it is exceptionally neat and well-organized. This resume is easily read, and key information is highly visible. Even though it spans close to 25 years, it can be read quickly and all relevant information is at the employer's fingertips.

When reviewing Resume H, you will note that each position held by the candidate is fully described, including reporting relationship, scope and size of position, and key job responsibilities. Likewise, for each position held, there is some description of major accomplishments or results achieved by the candidate.

Resume H—Good Resume

WARREN B. SLOAN
825 Summit Avenue
Wyomissing, PA 19872

Phone: (215) 775-0967

OBJECTIVE:

Senior level position in Operations management in medium-sized manufacturing company.

EDUCATION:

M.S., Pennsylvania State University, 1978
Major: Mechanical Engineering

B.S., Pennsylvania State University, 1976
Major: Mechanical Engineering
Grade Point Average: 3.7/4.0
Tau Beta Psi

EXPERIENCE:

1988
to
Pres.

WELLINGTON TUBE CORPORATION

Vice President of Manufacturing – Corporate Offices (1992 to Present)
Report to President of this leading, $500 million manufacturer of copper tubing. Full P&L responsibility for operation of two state-of-the-art copper refineries and tube manufacturing facilities ($300 million budget, 5,000 hourly employees, 300 salaried employees).

Achievements:

* Directed cost reduction task force achieving 22% reduction in operating costs in 3 years ($60 million annual savings).

* Installed raw materials & inventory control computer system cutting raw materials inventories by 30% ($15 million annual savings).

* Implemented "high performance work system" resulting in increased employee participation and 10% productivity improvement.

Plant Manager – Norfolk Plant (1988-1992)
Reported to Vice President of Manufacturing with P&L responsibility for this 3,000 employee copper refinery and tube manufacturing plant ($375 million annual production). Functional accountability included manufacturing, distribution, engineering, maintenance, materials management, accounting and human resources.

Resume H —(Continued)

Achievements:

* Led successful $125 capital expansion program, doubling plant capacity (completed on-time and 10% under budget).

* Directed work redesign project (with union as partner), reducing job classifications from 42 to 15 and resulting in agreement to reduce plant headcount by 10% over 3 years.

* Set plant production and safety records for 4 straight years (1989 through 1992).

1983
to
1988

DOBBLER COPPER COMPANY, INC. (CORPORATE OFFICES)

Manager of Engineering
Reported to Vice President of Operations of this $250 million manufacturer of refrigeration tubing. Directed 150 employee central engineering function with responsibility for all capital expansion projects to include engineering design, installation, start-up and debugging of copper tube refining/and manufacturing facilities.

Achievements:

* Successfully led $125 million capital expansion program (largest in company's history) in the engineering and start-up of major, state-of-the-art, computer controlled, fully-integrated copper refining and manufacturing facility (program completed on time and under budget).

* Reorganized and streamlined central engineering function, reducing headcount by 21% with no appreciable drop in department productivity ($1.5 million annual savings).

1978
to
1983

ZACKRISON COPPER & BRASS COMPANY (BRISTOL PLANT)

Department Manager – Drawing Operation (1981-1983)
Reported to Plant Manager with responsibility for management of 100 employee, $85 million tube drawing operation.

Achievements:

* Implemented SPC-based "Total Quality" effort resulting in 48% scrap reduction ($2.1 million annual savings).

* Reduced employee annual turnover from 10% to 1.5% in 2 year period ($1.5 million annual savings).

Project Engineer (1978-1981)
Reported to Plant Operations Manager with responsibility for design, installation and start-up of major capital projects in furnace and drawing operations. Independently handled projects in the $10-15 million range.

There is thus a good balance between functional description and accomplishments, suggesting someone who is well-motivated and results-oriented.

Hopefully, this chapter has convinced you of the importance of a good resume to your overall job hunting campaign. The ensuing chapters will now walk you through each of the steps necessary to prepare an effective resume. Focus will be on the two most popular formats—the reverse chronological resume and the functional resume.

5

Preparing to Write the Resume

For most people, the task of writing a resume does not come easily. It is, at best, an unnatural process. There are few times in our lives when we are required to write about ourselves, and many find this an embarrassing process. By contrast, we are frequently called upon to write various business letters and reports. This is a process that most of us find considerably easier.

Taking a few moments to reflect on what is causing this anxiety will usually yield some fairly consistent answers as follows:

1. Lack knowledge of resume content (what to say or not say)

2. Lack knowledge of proper format (how to organize the resume)

3. Lack knowledge of proper style (how to express it).

If you know what to say, how to organize it, and how to express it, there should be little reason to feel uncomfortable about the resume process. In addition, the more you have prepared and rehearsed, the more comfortable you will feel in your ability to write a suitable resume. This chapter is designed to assist you in developing these preparation skills, and the confidence to move on to the actual writing.

Moreover, the direction of this chapter will be twofold. First, we will focus on systematically gathering the necessary data about you and your background. Second, we will focus on writing skills, i.e., how to word the resume to achieve maximum effectiveness. The subject of format (how to organize the resume) will be dealt with in the subsequent chapters on the chronological and functional resumes.

PERSONAL DATA

Before you can proceed with the actual process of resume writing, you will need to have a considerable amount of personal data at your fingertips. Further, these facts must be organized in such a manner as to be easily accessible when you need them. This advance preparation is essential to assuring an orderly, efficient resume process. It is intended to save you time and frustration.

The forms provided at the end of this chapter have been designed to assist you in systematically collecting the key information that you will need to have available once the actual writing process begins.

Professional Experience

Directions using the "Experience" section of the forms provided at the end of this chapter, start with your most recent employer and list all previous employment: dates of employment, name of employer, division for which you worked, title of position held, title of person to whom you reported, job description (functional responsibilities and size/scope of position), and major accomplishments.

In those cases where you held more than one position with the same employer, write the word *same* in the space provided for the employer's name. Also, in those cases where you have held more than six positions, continue with this exercise on a separate piece of paper.

Unless you are a student, don't list summer jobs or part-time employment. Students, however, should include all summer, co-op, intern and part-time positions.

By completing these forms you will have collected the basic information that you will need to have available for the preparation of your resume. This same information should also prove helpful as you approach your employment interview (discussed later in this book).

POWER WRITING

Let's move from discussing resume content (what goes into the resume) to resume writing (how it is expressed). Writing style is a critical factor in the resume preparation process for three reasons:

1. Clarity—Information needs to be conveyed in a clear, concise manner that fosters good understanding and favorable communication.

2. Conciseness—Several years of experience need to be effectively condensed into a one or two-page format.

3. Forcefulness—Your message needs to be strong. It should have maximum impact in a minimum amount of space.

The art of saying things in a clear, concise and forceful manner is what I call *power writing*. Power writing is a strongly recommended technique that can give you the edge when competing with the myriad of resume an employer must read.

Let's examine some of the basic principles of power writing. Having considered these principles, we will then review some examples of power writing to demonstrate their effectiveness and importance in resume writing.

Rules of Power Writing

The fundamental rules of power writing are a follows:

1. Job Title—Avoid repeating your job title when describing your responsibilities and accomplishments. This is unnecessary since your title has already been stated as part of the resume heading.

2. Pronoun "I"—Avoid using the pronoun "I" in the text of your resume. Since this is your resume, the "I" is understood.

3. Action Verbs—Where possible, start sentences with an action verb followed by a noun or an adjective. This forces brevity and conciseness.

4. Incomplete Sentences—In resume writing, it is not always necessary to write in complete sentences to communicate effectively. This is particularly true since, in resume writing, the pronoun "I" is understood. The use of descriptive phrases and clauses is acceptable as long as they convey a complete thought and are clearly understood.

5. Condense/Consolidate—Where possible, condense related information into a single statement rather than making separate statements. Eliminate all nonessential information which adds little or no meaning to your employment qualifications.

6. Quantitative Descriptions—Where possible, use quantitative terms to describe your position and accomplishments.

This provides a sense of dimension or magnitude that is helpful in conveying fuller understanding and also makes the resume far more interesting to read.

Action Words

The following is a list of commonly used action words for resume writing, which should prove helpful as a reference to you during the writing process:

Managed	Conducted	Composed	Structured
Administered	Approved	Developed	Organized
Directed	Implemented	Founded	Planned
Supervised	Controlled	Created	Consolidated
Lead	Coordinated	Invented	Originated
Guided	Motivated	Conceived	Designed
Solved	Evaluated	Produced	Improved
Optimized	Revised	Designed	Streamlined
Scheduled	Modified	Built	Accelerated
Maximized	Analyzed	Generated	Expanded
Monitored	Researched	Engineered	Increased
Proved	Revamped	Provided	Saved
Maintained	Trained	Decreased	Instructed
Sold	Accomplished	Completed	Presented
Began	Provided	Eliminated	Negotiated
Purchased	Performed	Finished	Contracted
Launched	Expedited	Canceled	Taught
Established	Delivered	Reduced	Demonstrated

Power Writing Examples

The following are examples of how power writing can improve the wording and general impact of a resume. Both right and wrong examples are provided so that you can directly compare them. Note how the power writing rules, described earlier, are used to increase resume effectiveness.

Wrong

I reported to the Plant Manager. I was responsible for the maintenance, engineering and procurement departments, and managed a total of 150 hourly employees. I was also responsible for managing the plant's stockroom and being sure that we didn't run out of spare parts.

Right

Reported directly to Plant Manager of this 2,000-employee paper manufacturing plant. Managed the maintenance, engineering and procurement functions (150 employees, $12 million budget). Directed $35 million capital expansion project which doubled plant production and reduced operating costs by 10%. Installed computerized spare parts system, reducing spare parts inventory by 25% ($1.3 million annual savings).

Wrong

I reported to the Director of Administrative Personnel. I was responsible for managing the compensation, benefits, employment and training functions. My major accomplishments included the installation of human resources computer system and new executive bonus program. I also managed the organization effectiveness function and contributed to the increased effectiveness of the corporate distribution function through use of modern organization effectiveness techniques.

Right

Reported to Director of Administrative Personnel of this Fortune 100 personal care and cleaning products company. Managed compensation, benefits, employment, organization effectiveness and training functions (35 employees, $12.6 million budget). Installed human resources computer system, reducing H.R. staff by 10% (annual savings $320 thousand). Led O.E. effort that reduced corporate distribution operating costs by $48 million annually.

As can be seen from these examples, power writing can sub-stantially improve the overall impact of the employment re-sume. Now, complete the following forms. Remember to use the power writing techniques described in this chapter when com-pleting the "Experience" section. Some careful attention to proper wording and use of the power writing techniques at this stage, will serve to save you considerable time later when you actually write your resume.

Education

Starting with your most recent degree, fill in each of the spaces provided.

1. Degree   _____
   School   _____   Date graduated _____
   Major   _____   Grade point average _____
   Minor   _____   Grade point average _____
   Honoraries   _____
                  _____
                  _____
   Scholarships   _____
                  _____
                  _____
   Publications   _____
                  _____
                  _____
   Offices held   _____
                  _____
                  _____

2. Degree   _____
   School   _____   Date graduated _____

Major   _____ Grade point average _____

Minor   _____ Grade point average _____

Honoraries   _____

                        _____

                        _____

Scholarships   _____

                        _____

                        _____

Publications   _____

                        _____

                        _____

Offices held   _____

                        _____

                        _____

Experience

1. Dates Employed   From _____ to _____

   Employer   _____

   Division   _____

   Position title   _____

   Reported to   _____

   Responsibilities   _____

_____

_____

_____

_____

_____

_____

_____

Accomplishments _____

_____

_____

_____

_____

_____

2. Dates Employed   From _____ to _____

    Employer   _____

    Division   _____

    Position title   _____

    Reported to   _____

    Responsibilities   _____

_____

_____

_____

_____

_____

    Accomplishments   _____

_____

_____

_____

_____

_____

3. Dates Employed   From _____ to _____

    Employer   _____

    Division   _____

Position title   _____

Reported to   _____

Responsibilities   _____

_____

_____

_____

_____

_____

_____

Accomplishments   _____

_____

_____

_____

_____

_____

4. Dates Employed   From _____ to _____

   Employer   _____

   Division   _____

   Position title   _____

   Reported to   _____

   Responsibilities _____

_____

_____

_____

_____

_____

_____

Accomplishments _____

_____

_____

_____

_____

_____

_____

5. Dates Employed   From _____ to _____

   Employer   _____

   Division   _____

   Position title   _____

   Reported to   _____

   Responsibilities   _____

   _____

   _____

   _____

   _____

   _____

   _____

   Accomplishments _____

   _____

   _____

   _____

   _____

   _____

   _____

6. Dates Employed   From _____ to _____

   Employer   _____

   Division   _____

   Position title   _____

   Reported to   _____

   Responsibilities   _____

_____

_____

_____

_____

_____

_____

   Accomplishments   _____

_____

_____

_____

_____

_____

_____

Professional Credentials

Professional Certification

   Professional certification license _____

   Date certified or licensed   _____

   Certifying organization _____

   Professional certification license _____

   Date certified or licensed   _____

   Certifying organization _____

Professional Memberships

    Name of organization   ————————————————————

    Membership dates   From ——————— to ———————

    Offices held   ————————————————————

       ————————————————————

       ————————————————————

    Name of organization   ————————————————————

    Membership dates   From ——————— to ———————

    Offices held   ————————————————————

       ————————————————————

       ————————————————————

    Name of organization   ————————————————————

    Membership dates   From ——————— to ———————

    Offices held   ————————————————————

       ————————————————————

       ————————————————————

Military Service

Dates served   From ——————— to ———————

Branch of service   ————————————————————

Unit   ————————————————————

Rank at discharge   ————————————————————

Date of discharge   ————————————————————

Type of discharge   ————————————————————

6

Resume Style — Picking the Right One

Most employment authorities would agree that there are essentially only two basic resume formats that are worth your consideration—the chronological and the functional. Combined, they probably account for 80 to 85 percent of all resumes received by employers. Having to contend with just these two popular formats will make the selection process a lot simpler than some would have you think.

There is, perhaps, one major exception to this simple choice. In the case of those seeking employment in professions requiring a high level of creativity (i.e., artists or designers) there may be some benefit to a more inventive, unique approach. This book, however, does not attempt to deal with unusual cases such as these. To do so would benefit only a very small portion of the work-eligible population, and create confusion at a time when understanding and clarity of mission are essential to effective resume preparation.

BEWARE OF WOULD-BE EXPERTS

Sadly for the job seeker, and would-be resume writer, there is a proliferation of bad advice on the subject of resume preparation. It seems that the world abounds with self-proclaimed experts on this subject, and they are all too willing to share their misinformation with any unsuspecting soul who is unfortunate enough to listen.

I am always amazed by the *credentials* of these "experts," many of whom have little or no relevant employment experience. All too often, because of their educational background, standing in the community, business position, or other tangible evidence of success, it is assumed by the unwary job hunter that these persons are truly knowledgeable about the subject of professional resume preparation. Frequently, however, nothing could be further from the truth! This unfortunate counsel is perpetuated by the fact that many of these well-intentioned amateurs truly believe in the advice they are prescribing to their unwitting audience.

Regrettably, resume preparation is one of those topics, like politics or religion, that practically everyone feels they know something about. Just ask, and you are bound to get an earful of guidance—most of it bad. If you are tempted to ask others for advice on this subject, or are about to buy a book on the subject, I have one admonition—*consider the source!*

Would you go to your barber for accounting suggestions? Your car dealer for real estate tips? Your attorney for spiritual help? Of course you wouldn't! Then why entrust a novice with something as important as preparation of your employment resume? After all, the quality of your resume could have significant impact on your current job hunting prospects, as well as your entire career. Why not be sure, then, that the person who advises you in this area is someone who is qualified to do so.

Here are some recommended questions to consider to be sure that you are dealing with a knowledgeable source:

1. How much actual employment experience has this person had?

2. How many actual persons has this individual been responsible for hiring? A few? Several hundred?

3. Has this person been responsible for hiring only into a narrowly-defined functional specialty (e.g., accounting, law, engineering, etc.); or has the employment experience spanned a wide range of functional disciplines?

4. Has this person's hiring experience been limited to only certain levels within the hiring organization (e.g., college entry level, professional level, middle management, top management, etc.), or has it transcended all organizational levels?

5. Importantly, how much resume reading has this person actually done? Does he/she read all or most of the resumes, or are the bulk of these read by someone else?

6. Is this the person who, having read the resume, makes the preliminary decision on which persons to invite in for interviews, or is this the person who merely reviews the resumes of those finalists whose resumes have been prescreened by someone else?

There are many would-be authorities in the business of dispensing resume advice. Yours is the challenge of distinguishing between the seasoned expert and the well-intentioned novice. Hopefully, the questions I have posed will provide you with the necessary ammunition to draw a clear distinction between these two groupings. The effectiveness of your resume and overall job search success may be riding on this important distinction, and whose advice you elect to follow.

WHAT THE EXPERTS RECOMMEND

Review of current literature on the subject of resumes reveals that experienced employment professionals (the experts) are in general agreement concerning what constitutes an acceptable resume format. Depending upon the job seeker's particular circumstances, these experts unanimously agree that there are essentially only two acceptable, recommended choices. These are:

1. The chronological format

2. The functional format

Unlike several of the unqualified resume counselors, these employment experts *do not recommend the use of unique or unconventional resume styles.* By contrast, many non-experts would have you believe that such uniqueness will "set you apart from the masses, and the prospective employer will single you out for your brilliance and creative genius." "Nonsense," say the employment professionals. "Such advice will only expose you for the gullible sap that you really are and guarantee that your resume will go forth into the endlessness of eternal oblivion."

In a more serious vein, use of an unconventional format may suggest one or more of the following to the true employment professional:

1. The applicant is ignorant of proper resume protocol.

2. The applicant lacks knowledge of commonly accepted business practice.

3. The applicant lacks good business judgment.

4. The applicant lacks good taste.

5. The applicant resists conformity, resents authority, and may be a malcontent.

6. The applicant is a lone wolf, not a team player.

Conversely, use of a proper resume format can suggest just the opposite:

1. The applicant is knowledgeable of proper resume protocol.
2. The applicant is knowledgeable of commonly accepted business practice.
3. The applicant exercises good business judgment.
4. The applicant demonstrates sound judgment and good taste.
5. The applicant respects conventional authority and is well-adjusted.
6. The applicant is likely cooperative and a good team player.

Thus, most employment experts would agree that there are really only two viable resume choices—the chronological format and the functional format. Use of any other style by you is to flirt with probable resume and possible job search failure. At best, you will likely lose resume effectiveness and generally detract from your employment candidacy. At worst, you could kill your employment campaign before it even gets started.

Why take this chance when you can substantially improve your overall job search effectiveness through use of a proven, acceptable resume style?

Let's now examine these two recommended styles. In doing so, we will consider the following questions:

Chronological Format

1. What is the chronological resume?
2. What does it look like?
3. What are its advantages?
4. What are its disadvantages?
5. When should it be used?
6. When should it be avoided?

Functional Format

1. What is the functional resume?

2. What does it look like?

3. What are its advantages?

4. What are its disadvantages?

5. When should it be used?

6. When should it be avoided?

THE CHRONOLOGICAL FORMAT

Take a moment to review the sample chronological resume on page 100. What makes this a chronological format is the fact that the "Experience" section lists the positions held in a chronological sequence, starting with the most recent and working back to the individual's first professional job. So, technically, this particular format is really a *reverse chronological resume*, and some prefer this terminology since it is a more accurate description. (For the sake of continuity, however, this book will use the term *chronological resume* in its reference to this format.)

The chronological resume is by far the most popular and widely used resume format. It represents an estimated 60 to 65 percent of all resumes received by employers. Without a doubt, it is the resume style most preferred by seasoned employment experts. With few exceptions, which are carefully explained later, I therefore strongly recommend the use of this particular format about all others.

Advantages of Chronological Format

There are excellent reasons to choose the chronological resume. These are as follows:

1. Since it is the most commonly used, it is the format with which employers are most familiar and feel the most comfortable.

2. The chronological format provides for a logical, easy-to-read flow with point-to-point continuity from one employment position and employer to the next.

3. This same logical flow makes it one of the easiest resumes to prepare.

4. This format allows the job hunter to emphasize career growth and progression (where he/she has experienced such)—two factors viewed favorably by most employers.

5. Likewise, this format serves to highlight continuity of employment (employer/job stability) and career continuity—both considered desirable factors by most employers.

6. This format also serves to highlight names of past employers, which can be advantageous where some or all of these are well-known, prestigious companies.

Disadvantages of Chronological Format

Although by far the most preferred resume style, the chronological format is not without its disadvantages for a small percentage of job seekers. And, there are certain circumstances which may dictate that it not be used at all. Possible disadvantages include:

1. This format can serve to highlight obvious employment handicaps, including:
   a. Job hopping
   b. Employment gaps
   c. Underemployment
   d. Lack of career progress
   e. Little or no related work experience
   f. Age

2. Can tend to draw attention to career progression, rather than to specific personal or functional strengths.

3. Can tend to highlight most recent experience, when, in some cases certain earlier experiences may be more relevant to current job search objective.

4. Can tend to short-change certain key accomplishments, when these occurred earlier in the career and are relevant to the current job search objective.

When to Use Chronological Format

The following is provided as a guideline for determining when to use the chronological format:

1. This format is strongly recommended when all of the following factors exist:
   a. Reasonable/good career continuity.
   b. Reasonable/good career progression.
   c. Reasonable/good job stability.

   (You may want to carefully consider using the functional format instead, if any of these factors rank at the "poor" level.)

2. When recent employment history is related to/supportive of current job search objective.

3. When overall employment experience is related to/supportive of current job hunting objective.

When Not to Use Chronological Format

There are times when the chronological resume may not be appropriate to achieve maximum effectiveness. The following guideline is provided to assist you in making this determination:

1. This format is not recommended when one or more of the following apply:

   a. Poor career continuity (i.e., there have been several changes in career direction).

   b. Little or no career progression (i.e., career has stagnated and there have been no promotions or advancement over an extended time period).

   c. Poor record of employment stability (i.e., four or more employers in last ten years; seven or more employers during professional career).

2. This format is generally inappropriate when recent employment history is unrelated to current job objective (unless such unrelated employment was of relatively short duration and was immediately preceded by relevant work experience).

3. The chronological format is also not indicated when there is little or no related work experience (i.e., career change).

4. This resume style would be inappropriate where there have been significant or frequent gaps in employment (i.e., unemployed for more than one year in last ten years; unemployed two or more times in the last five years).

5. The chronological format is not normally recommended when there has been an extended period of underemployment immediately prior to the job search (i.e., a significant reduction in job scope, level, and responsibility that has lasted one year or more).

6. This format is less than ideal when earlier employment experience is clearly more relevant to the current job target than are positions held in the recent past.

7. This style resume may be less appropriate when relevant key accomplishments occurred earlier in the career.

Chronological Resume

DAVID B. SAMPSON
325 Smithbridge Road
Old Forge, PA 19872

Phone: (215) 872-8725

OBJECTIVE:

Senior level management position in financial planning.

EDUCATION:

M.B.A., University of Chicago, 1982
Major: Finance
Grade Point Average: 3.8/4.0
Class Rank: 8/165
Brasston Fellowship, 1980-1982

B.A., University of Wisconsin, 1980
Major: Business Administration
Grade Point Average: 3.9/4.0
Summa Cum Laude

EXPERIENCE:

1985
to
Pres.

STARDAN MANUFACTURING, INC. (CORPORATE OFFICES)

Chief Financial Officer (1990 to Present)
Report to President of this Fortune 200, $3.8 billion manufacturer of industrial valves and fittings. Functional accountabilities include: business development, financial planning, finance, accounting and information services. Manage 325 employee staff, $22 million budget, and $2.7 billion corporate debt portfolio.

Achievements:

* Secured ten-year financing of $1.6 billion capital program at 1% below prime rate ($16 million annual savings).

* Acquired $80 million speciality value manufacturer with first year net return of 14% ($11.2 million profit).

* Led successful installation of $5 million order entry, tracking and automatic invoicing computer system ($2.7 million annual savings).

Director of Strategic Planning (1985-1990)
Reported to Chief Financial Officer, with functional responsibility for business development and strategic planning (28 professionals, $1.6 million budget).

Chronological Resume (Continued)

Achievements:

* Directed development of first believable, five-year strategic planning computer model (60% timesaving on annual planning process).

* Managed full acquisition analysis and recommendations on 18 acquisition candidates.

* Directed successful acquisition of 4 target companies ($185 million).

1982
to
1985

BARRINGTON CORPORATION (CORPORATE OFFICES)

Senior Financial Planner (1984-1985)
Reported to Director of Financial Planning of this $1.7 billion manufacturer of of printed circuit boards.

Achievements:

* Developed financial planning strategy to fund annual capital requirements of $100 to $125 million.

* Successfully negotiated $45 million loan for French affiliate at highly favorable rate and term.

Financial Planner (1983-1984)
Reported to Director of Financial Planning. Planned funding strategy for an $85 million capital expansion project.

Financial Analyst (1982-1983)
Reported to a Senior Financial Planner. Responsible for determination of capital funding requirements for various capital projects.

THE FUNCTIONAL FORMAT

Take a moment to review the sample functional resume on page 104. The functional resume, as you will notice, highlights the employment candidate's background and accomplishments under broad functional categories. Categories chosen for emphasis are normally functional area (i.e., cost accounting, market research, labor relations, finance, sales management, etc.). In each case, selected major accomplishments and results are then delineated under these key functional headings. Normally, these functions are listed in descending order based upon their relevance to the current job hunting objective. Thus, the most pertinent factors are listed first, with less germane points falling further down in the listing.

The functional resume format is the second most popular resume and represents an estimated 20 to 25 percent of all resumes received by employers. Although popular among job seekers, the functional format is far less popular with employers and with good reason. It is strongly recommended, therefore, that this resume style not be used by you unless absolutely necessary. The rule of thumb is, *When in doubt, use the chronological format.* Let's take a look at the advantages and disadvantages of the functional resume format.

Advantages of Functional Format

With the exception of the chronological resume format, there are some good reasons to prefer the functional format over other less conventional resume styles. Key advantages of this format are as follows:

1. Since it is the second most commonly used resume style, it is a format with which most employers are familiar and feel somewhat comfortable.

2. This format allows you to highlight the most relevant, job-related aspects of your background (i.e., functional experience, skills, accomplishments, etc.) even though these key qualifications are more evident from positions held earlier in your career.

3. Since it is not chronologically constrained, this resume style allows you the flexibility of listing your most apropos qualifications first, thus drawing maximum attention to them.

4. The functional resume format provides the opportunity to de-emphasize, or otherwise camouflage, a multitude of undesirable circumstances such as:
   a. Lack of career progress
   b. Lack of career continuity
   c. Job hopping
   d. Lengthy/frequent unemployment
   e. Lack of required experience
   f. Lack of required education
   g. Age

5. A functional format, which emphasizes key skills and capabilities, may suggest to the employer that there is more than one job where your overall qualifications could be utilized.

Disadvantages of the Functional Format

With the preceding list of advantages, it may be hard to imagine that there are many disadvantages to using the functional resume format. However, this format does have some very real disadvantages that can substantially outweigh its advantages. These disadvantages are the very same ones that cause most employers and employment professionals to strongly recommend that job applicants use the chronological resume format. It is because of these same handicaps that I encourage careful thought and analysis

Functional Resume

DAVID B. SAMPSON
325 Smithbridge Road
Old Forge, PA 19872

Phone: (215) 872-8725

SUMMARY:

Seasoned financial executive with 12 years progressive management experience
in all major financial functions: finance, financial planning, business development
accounting and information services. Excellent record of advancement and strong
contributor to bottom line results.

ACCOMPLISHMENTS:

Financial Planning

* Directed all financial functions for Fortune 200 manufacturing company ($3.8 billion
  annual sales).

* Directed long and short-term planning for $2.7 billion corporate debt portfolio.

* Developed long-term financial planning computer model to forecast five-year capital
  requirements within plus or minus 2%.

* Planned capital funding strategy for annual capital requirements in the $100 to $125
  million range.

Finance

* Directed all financing (short & long-term) of $2.7 billion corporate debt portfolio.

* Financed $1.6 billion capital program at 1% below prime rate ($16 million annual
  savings).

* Financed $80 million acquisition with first year net return of 14% ($11.2 million
  profit).

* Negotiated all financing to support acquisition of 4 target companies (highly
  favorable rates & terms).

Acquisitions

* Directed identification, analysis, negotiation and successful acquisition of 4 highly
  desirable target companies.

* Directed complete analysis and recommendations on 18 acquisition candidates in 2
  years.

Functional Resume (Continued)

EXPERIENCE:

1987	**Stardan Manufacturing, Inc. (Corporate Offices)**	
to	Chief Financial Officer	(1992 to Present)
Pres.	Director of Strategic Planning	(1987-1992)

1982	**Barrington Corporation (Corporate Offices)**	
to	Senior Financial Planner	(1985-1987)
1987	Financial Planner	(1983-1985)
	Financial Analyst	(1982-1983)

EDUCATION:

M.B.A., University of Chicago, 1982
Major: Finance
Grade Point Average: 3.8/4.0
Class Rank: 8/165
Brasston Fellowship, 1980-1982

B.A., University of Wisconsin, 1980
Major: Business Administration
Grade Point Average: 3.9/4.0
Summa Cum Laude

before deciding to use the functional format. Remember, *When in doubt, use the chronological format.*

Major disadvantages of the functional resume format are as follows:

1. This format arouses immediate suspicion on the part of employers. Most employers are keenly aware that it is the format most frequently used by applicants who have something to hide, such as:
   a. Lack of career progress
   b. Lack of career continuity
   c. Frequent changes of job/employer
   d. Lengthy/frequent unemployment
   e. Lack of required experience
   f. Lack of required education
   g. Age

   This elicits a negative attitude right from the beginning, and the employer commences resume reading as if on a witch hunt—focusing attention on searching out the problem, rather than on the candidate's qualifications for the position.

2. This format is difficult to read and often creates confusion. The lack of logical continuity and completeness leaves the employer guessing about certain key factors important to the employment decision-making process. This leaves the employer with only one option—to call the candidate for clarification. Busy employment professionals won't even bother; they just move on to the next candidate's resume.

3. The functional format can frustrate the employer. Since there is no linkage provided between specific positions held, and functional experience and results, the employer becomes easily thwarted in his or her attempt to make these connections. This sets off a negative, rather than a positive, attitude toward the job applicant.

4. Generally, this format is more difficult to prepare when compared to the chronological resume format, where there is a more logical job-by-job continuity of thought.

When to Use the Functional Format

Considering the disadvantages, you may be somewhat confused about when you should choose the functional format over the chronological. Hopefully, you will find the following guideline helpful when making this determination.

The functional resume format should be used when:

1. There is some major, negative information that, if highlighted or disclosed, would almost certainly preclude further consideration of your employment candidacy. Examples of such *knock-out factors* are:

   a. Major career stagnation (i.e., no promotions or expansion of job responsibilities in last six years).

   b. Obvious lack of career continuity (i.e., frequent, continuous changes in career direction).

   c. Frequent changes of jobs/employers (i.e., four employers in ten years, seven or more employers during career, three or more recent jobs averaging less than two years duration, or, three or more jobs during career that were less than one year duration).

   d. Lengthy or frequent periods of unemployment (i.e., unemployed for more than one year in last ten years, two or more periods of at least yearlong unemployment, or, one period of two-year unemployment).

   e. Lack of critical experience considered essential to position.

   f. Lack of required education (unless there is sufficient relevant experience to offset this requirement).

2. When critical skills and capabilities would not be sufficiently evident from use of a standard chronological format (i.e., skills/capabilities were acquired through life experiences other than professional career employment).

3. When recent employment history is totally unrelated, or only distantly related, to current job search objective, and earlier work experience is clearly more relevant.

4. When there has been a period of substantial underemployment (i.e., a significant reduction in job scope, level or responsibility) that has lasted for more than one year. (Note: Dependent upon the magnitude and duration of this reduction, it may still be advisable to use the chronological format, simply providing a brief description of this lesser position.)

5. When your career objective is not clearly defined and you wish to stress your overall skills and capabilities so that the employer might consider your qualifications for several areas. (Note: This is a very ineffective way to go to market, and substantially reduces the probability of a successful job hunting campaign.)

When Not to Use the Functional Format

The functional resume format should not be used under these circumstances:

1. When there has been reasonable/good career progression.

2. When there has been reasonable/good career continuity (as well as career progression).

3. Where there has been a reasonable/good history of employment stability (provided such stability is coupled with reasonable/good career progression and career continuity).

4. Where career history is void of lengthy or frequent periods of unemployment (and items 1, 2, and 3 are also satisfactory).

5. Where critical work experience requirements (as well as items 1 through 4) are satisfied.

GENERAL OBSERVATIONS

As you can see from this discussion, selection of a proper resume format is not a cut-and-dried decision. It requires some careful thought and consideration if you are going to select the format that will be most beneficial to you.

The disadvantages of using the functional resume format, in the great majority of cases, outweigh those of the standard chronological format. At the risk of sounding like a broken record, the rule of thumb is, *when in doubt, use the chronological format.*

A WORD ABOUT RESUME APPEARANCE

Putting the subject of resume format aside, it is worthwhile to understand that the general appearance of the employment resume is very important to the job hunting campaign. Think of the resume as an extension of you. If it is neat, crisp, and well-organized, it will suggest to the employer that you are someone who is careful and concerned about the quality of your work. A sloppy, disorganized resume, conversely, will create an unfavorable impression with prospective employers and greatly hinder, if not ruin, your employment efforts. It is imperative, therefore, that you be attentive to the general appearance of your resume document, and that you take the necessary steps to make a favorable impression.

Here are some suggestions to improve the physical appearance and, therefore, the overall effectiveness of your resume:

1. Use a high quality bond paper in either white or buff.

2. Carefully proofread and edit to ensure proper spelling, grammar, punctuation, and comprehension. (If necessary, seek help from a professional.)

3. Have your resume professionally typed. At a cost of only a few dollars a page, you can hardly afford not to. This is a minor investment considering your entire career is at stake.

4. Have your typist advise you on proper style type. Avoid unusual or unique typefaces.

5. Make effective use of highlighting (bold type) and underlining to facilitate ease of reading and appropriate topical emphasis. (Note the sample resume in this book for proper use of both, and tailor your resume accordingly.)

6. Avoid ragged or uneven margins. Use of right margin justification by your typist will greatly enhance the appearance.

7. Make sure that final copy is neat, well-space, uncluttered and easy to read.

8. Final printing should be done on a quality laser jet printer or by a professional printer using quality photo-offset printing equipment.

Although all of this may seem like basic advice, it is surprising what a high percentage of resumes don't meet these simple standards. What a shame, when it is so easy to improve the general appearance and overall effectiveness of this vital document. The extra effort can have substantial payoff for your job hunting campaign.

Since we have now completed a fairly indepth discussion concerning resume format and appearance (and you have likely made the choice between using a chronological or a functional resume format), we can now move on to actual resume preparation. The next two chapters show how to effectively prepare these two formats. Several examples of each of these styles are also provided. Chapter 7 deals with the chronological format; Chapter 8 covers the functional format. Choose the appropriate chapter and proceed with actual preparation of your resume document.

7

Writing the Chronological Resume

This chapter will deal with preparation of the chronological resume format. I will walk you through each major component of the resume and provide you with appropriate instructions for its preparation. As each resume section is discussed, I will attempt to answer three basic questions. These questions are:

1. How should the resume section be written?

2. What should the section contain?

3. What should be excluded from the section?

SOME GENERAL OBSERVATIONS

Before you get started with this chapter and the preparation of your own resume, I strongly recommend that you take a few minutes to carefully study the several resume samples contained at the end of the Chapter. There are several general observations that need to be made concerning the overall appearance of the resume. They are:

1. Note that the candidate's name is capitalized in bold type, and all major sectional headings (objective, education, experience, military service etc.) are printed in capital letters, bold type and underlined. This serves to highlight these sections, provides for ease of reading and facilitates the quick location of key information.

2. Note the positioning of dates in the Experience section of the resume. Dates representing the total period of employment with each employer are positioned at the left hand margin. On the other hand, employment dates for each position held with these employers are shown in brackets to the right of their respective title. Visually separating the dates in this fashion avoids confusion concerning which positions were held with which employers. This also draws attention to employment stability rather than the perception of job hopping, which can happen when both the employer and position dates are listed together in the same column at the left margin of the resume.

3. Note that the names of employers are in bold type, capitalized and underlined.

4. Note that all position titles are in bold type, are underlined and that the initial letters of each word in these titles are capitalized. This has the effect of visually subordinating the position title to the name of the employer, further reinforcing the impression of employment stability. It is also aesthetically pleasing and improves resume readability.

5. Note the use of spacing throughout the resume. Double spacing is used to separate each discrete segment to create readable units. Proper spacing enhances resume appearance and readability, and makes locating specific topics easy.

6. Note the neatness and alignment of both margins and tabs. You will also notice that the left margin of all text material contained under each major section, is completely aligned. Right margins have been justified, eliminating the ragged effect. This overall alignment adds substantially to the document's neat, crisp countenance and creates a very favorable impression.

7. Where possible, all text for each major resume section should appear on the same page. This also improves the look and readability. Depending on the length and positioning of the text, this may not be possible without either cramming too much text against the bottom of the page, or leaving an abnormal amount of space. Use your best judgment.

RESUME COMPONENTS

The basic components of the chronological resume are:

1. Heading

2. Objective

3. Education

4. Experience

5. Military service

Although these sections are standard, and included in all chronological resume formats, there are also some discretionary or optional components, which may or may not be included. In certain circumstances, it is recommended that these optional sections be included, and in other circumstances, it is specifically recommended that they be excluded. These discretionary components are:

1. Professional certification

2. Professional affiliations

3. Publications

4. Patents

5. Community service

6. Hobbies and activities

Guidelines concerning the use of these optional components can be found later in this chapter.

We will now proceed with a detailed description of each of the basic resume components. In general, with few exceptions, they will be presented in the same sequence that they normally appear on the employment resume. In this way, you can apply the advice given by simultaneously writing and developing each component of your own personal resume at the time it is discussed. The cumulative effect of following this procedure will be the completion of your resume by the time you have finished this chapter.

Don't forget all the background data that you formulated back in Chapter 5, *Preparing to Write the Resume.* You will want to draw information directly from the forms that you filled in. It is suggested that you take a moment to now review these forms.

HEADING

The resume heading is fairly simple and straightforward. It consists of your name (in capital letters and bold print), address and home telephone.

Office telephone number can also be included; however, this may cause some employers to wonder why you are willing to accept calls concerning employment at your place of work. This may suggest that you have already been terminated and are in an outplacement mode, or you have recently been given notice. It is advisable, therefore, that you consider excluding the office phone number from your resume, provided you can reasonably be reached at your home phone. Use of an answering service or phone answering machine during your job hunting campaign may offer a good solution to this problem.

OBJECTIVE

The objective portion of your resume is important since it is the area of the resume which is used to communicate both the level and type of position in which you would be interested. Without such a statement, employers are uncertain whether current openings would be a match for your position requirements. If you are a dead ringer for a current opening, in most cases lack of an objective statement would have little or no effect. In such cases, the employer will likely be calling you to discuss the position.

The problem comes when you would appear to have only some of the qualifications of the position. In such cases, lack of an objective statement could prove to be the one factor that knocks you out of contention for the position. When your job search objective aligns well with the employer's requirements, however, your chances of an interview are greatly improved.

It is essential that the objective statement be properly worded. If the objective is too narrowly focused, it could have the effect of screening you out of opportunities in which you could well have an interest. An objective that is *too broad* may suggest that you are vague or that you haven't given enough thought to your career. If you haven't given quality thought to something as important as your own career, how well will you handle the analytical and problem solving responsibilities of your job? This question is likely to be in the employer's mind, and could cast doubt on the viability of your employment candidacy.

To emphasize this point, consider the following two objective statements:

1. Objective: Chief Financial Officer of major company with functional accountability for finance, strategic planning, business development, accounting and information services.

2. Objective: Financial management position with major company.

The first objective statement is overly specific and might, therefore, have the effect of depriving the candidate of positions that may be of interest. For instance, use of the word *major* could cause the candidate, in this example, to be screened out by medium-sized and smaller companies. Likewise, the delineation of functional areas implies the candidate would only be interested in positions that included all of these functional areas. In such case, he/she might not be considered for a position as CFO for a company where the I.S. function did not report to this position.

The second objective statement, on the other hand, is stated so broadly that it is practically meaningless. Prospective employers are given no idea of the level and scope of the position sought. Without at least some parameters, it is difficult for the employer to determine whether a particular job opening is appropriate. Instead of taking the time to find out, the employer may just move on to the next resume in the pile, in search of qualified candidates whose objectives are a clear fit with their requirements.

So, as you can see, a well-stated objective is a vital element of the resume. Review some of the objective statements in the sample resumes found at the end of this chapter, and then try your hand at writing your own objective statement.

EDUCATION

Normally, the Education section of the resume should contain the following components in this sequence:

1. Line 1: Degree awarded, school and date of graduation

2. Line 2: Major (and minor, if applicable)

3. Line 3: Grade point average (List if 3.0/4.0 or higher; exclude if less than 3.0/4.0)

4. Line 4: Class rank (List if top 10%; exclude if lower than top 10%)

5. Line 5: Scholarships/fellowships and years awarded

6. Line 6: Honors/awards and years awarded

With the passage of time, educational credentials take on decreasing meaning, and professional work experience and capabilities become increasingly more important in the assessment of candidate qualifications. As a result, it is recommended that more heavily-experienced persons consider positioning the Education section of the resume immediately following the Experience section. Such positioning draws attention to experience and ability to contribute, rather than less relevant factors such as age. In fact, in the case of those over age 50, it is strongly recommended that you list only degree and school, and exclude date of graduation. Why make it easy for an employer to discriminate against you on the basis of age?

Age sensitivity is often dependent upon level in the organizational hierarchy. For example, an employer is less likely to be concerned about age when looking for a president than when in search of an entry level project engineer. Although equal opportunity laws have tempered the practice of age discrimination, we would be naive to think that such discrimination has been completely eliminated. So, if older, why highlight your age by listing education, including date of graduation, near the beginning of your resume?

The general guidelines for determining where to position the Education section of the resume are:

Position education before experience, if:

1. Your major and degree are related to/supportive of your job hunting objective.

2. You have graduated from a prestigious school (e.g., Harvard, Princeton, Yale, Columbia, Wharton, University of

Chicago, Stamford, M.I.T.), and you have a relevant degree and major.

3. Your overall academic credentials are job target related and are also fairly impressive (e.g., graduate of a good school with honors, recipient of prestigious scholarships/fellowships, recipient of several honors/awards).

4. Your degree is recent and relevant to your job search objective. (The exception to this is if you are an older worker and the degree that you have just completed is at the undergraduate level.)

5. You are young, with limited experience, and are not concerned with emphasizing your age by showing date of graduation.

6. Your age is appropriate to your job level and you thus have no concern about revealing your age by showing graduation date.

In general, list education before experience if your educational credentials are supportive of your job search objective, and your educational qualifications enhance, rather than detract from, your overall desirability as an employment candidate.

Position education after experience, if:

1. Your degree and specific major are unrelated to, and therefore not supportive of, your job search objective.

2. You lack a graduate degree, and this is an absolute or preferred requirement for the position you seek.

3. You lack a formal degree, and this is normally required for the kind of position you want.

4. You graduated some time ago (usually 10 years or more), and you did not attend a well-known school.

5. Your age is incongruent with your job level (suggesting career stagnation or lack of promotability), and you do not wish to draw attention to your age early in the resume by showing graduation date.

6. Your experience is generally more impressive and job target related than your educational credentials.

7. In general, your educational credentials are unrelated, unremarkable or in any other way detract from your desirability as an employment candidate for the position you seek.

The correct positioning of the Education section contributes to the overall success of the resume. Sometimes it can be as important as the actual content of the section itself. Be sure, therefore, to give it careful consideration.

It is now suggested that you review the Education sections of some of the resumes at the end of this chapter. Having done this, write the Education section for your own resume.

EXPERIENCE

For the experienced person, the Experience section is probably the single most important part of the employment resume. It is this portion on which the employer focuses to determine whether you have the specific experience, knowledge, and skills to perform the duties of the position for which you are being considered. It is very important, therefore, that you invest adequate time and effort to describe this aspect of your background particularly well.

In preparing the Experience section, it is helpful to try to place yourself in the employer's shoes. What kind of information does the employer need in order to evaluate your background and qualifications? This is the same information that you will want to provide in the Experience section.

The first category of information normally required is that which relates to your past employers. This includes:

1. Employment dates

2. Employer's name

3. Location employed

The second category of information normally sought by prospective employers concerns the specific positions held. This includes:

1. Position title

2. Dates position held (from—to)

3. Reporting relationship (title of person to whom you reported)

4. Company description (size, products, services)

5. Size/scope of position (quantitative description of position—people and budgets managed, dollars impacted, etc.)

6. Functional responsibilities (functions for which you were responsible and titles of those who reported to you)

7. Major accomplishments/results (quantitative description of key results achieved—dollars saved, efficiencies gained, etc.)

From the exercises that you previously completed in Chapter 5, most of this key information should already be at your fingertips. It is now a matter of organizing this data into a nice, logical flow for each of the positions that you have held. Remember to use the power writing skills that you also learned in Chapter 5, to dramatically improve the impact and effectiveness of this section of your resume.

Take a few minutes to review the Experience sections of the resumes contained at the end of this chapter, and then proceed with writing a full description of each of the positions which you have held, using this format. Note the consistency of approach used in describing positions in the sample resumes. When describing each position held, topics are introduced in almost the identical sequence as listed above (i.e., reporting relationship, company description, size, and scope of position, functional responsibilities and major accomplishments). Try to follow the same topical sequence and employ power writing techniques, when writing your own position descriptions. You should find that, in doing so, things will flow rather smoothly.

MILITARY SERVICE

If you are just being discharged from the military, or were recently discharged, and your military experience comprises the bulk of your employment history, you should include your military employment under the Experience portion of your resume. In this case, you will want to provide a full description of your various assignments and accomplishments, much the same as you would in describing civilian experience in the same section.

Should your military service have occurred some time ago, and assuming this experience has little relevance to the position you are seeking, this service experience should be reported on the resume under the heading Military Service, and should be treated fairly lightly. A format similar to the following should be used:

MILITARY SERVICE: United States Army, 1975–1976
2nd Battalion, Armoured Div.
First Lieutenant
Honorable Discharge, 6/2/76

You may want to exclude this resume section entirely if you are older and inclusion would invite the possibility of age discrimination.

This concludes the discussion on the basic components of the chronological resume. Most often, use of these basic components (i.e., Heading, Objective, Education, Experience, and Military Service) is all that is necessary to ensure a complete and professional resume. There are times, however, when consideration should be given to the possible inclusion of certain additional resume elements. These elements are: Professional Certification, Patents, Publications, Professional Affiliations, Community Service, and Hobbies/Activities. A discussion of each of these discretionary or optional elements follows. Also provided are some basic guidelines for your use in deciding whether these should be included or excluded from your resume.

PROFESSIONAL CERTIFICATION

Where you are employed in a professional capacity and your profession requires a certain body of technical knowledge and skill, it may be helpful to your employment campaign to be able to show that you have professional certification in your area of expertise. Citing such certification provides objective evidence to prospective employers that they are getting someone whose technical knowledge and skills are judged to be at an acceptable professional level. This is particularly important when the employer with whom you may be interviewing has no one on staff who has training in this particular specialty, and has no way of accessing your technical competence.

Professional Certification is normally positioned as a *stand alone* category on the resume, and should immediately follow the Education section. Elements to be included in the Professional Certification section are: professional designation, name of certifying agency, and date of certification. Some examples would be:

PROFESSIONAL
CERTIFICATION: Professional Engineer, New Jersey, May 12, 1982
Certified Public Accountant, Maine, May 2, 1976

PATENTS/PUBLICATIONS

Generally, if you are a scientist or engineer and have some patents and technical publications to your credit, this fact should be acknowledged on the resume. This is also true of publications, if you are a writer. How much information you provide, and how specific you should be, depends directly upon how related this work is to the type of position for which you are applying.

In those cases where patents and publications have little or no relevance to your job target, there is no point in listing them individually. This is also true if, in addition, these patents and publications are dated several years ago. In such case, it is suggested that they simply be shown under the single heading of Patents/Publications as follows:

PATENTS & PUBLICATIONS: 12 U.S. patents
24 Publications
2 Books

Although this information has little direct relationship to the absolute requirements of the position for which you are applying, it does suggest some positive things about you (i.e., you are creative, intelligent, technically knowledgeable, well-motivated, etc.). In most cases, this should prove beneficial to your overall image and employment efforts.

There is one exception, however. If you are a scientist or engineer with exceptionally strong technical credentials on the theoretical side, and are attempting to transition to a career requiring strong applied, hands-on skills, you may want to de-emphasize your theoretical skills by simply excluding any reference to patents and technical publications from your resume.

This is particularly true if you feel prospective employers might have a tendency to view you as too theoretical for the position for which you are applying.

Conversely, where patents and publications are relatively recent and are very much related to your job search target position, this information should clearly be included in the resume. In those cases where there are only a few patents and publications, these can be listed under the single heading Patents/Publications. Where there are several items to be listed in each of these categories, it is suggested that you use two separate headings, "Patents" and "Publications." These categories are usually positioned immediately after the Experience section. If the list of patents and publications is quite lengthy, exclude them from the body of the resume, and instead list them on a separate page, entitled Patents and Publications.

When listing patents individually, you should include U.S. patent number, patent title, and date of issuance. Likewise, when listing publications individually, you should include title of the article, name of the publication in which article appeared, volume number, and publication date.

PROFESSIONAL AFFILIATIONS

Listing membership in professional associations is clearly an option when preparing an employment resume. Simply having a membership in such organizations tells a prospective employer very little, if anything, about your technical skills and qualifications. It is merely testimony to the fact that you are professionally active. This certainly can't hurt, but it doesn't normally add anything particularly meaningful to your qualifications from an employer's perspective.

The best criteria for deciding whether to include this category is space. If you can't add this information without unduly crowding other more important sections, or if it would warrant an additional page, I would recommend excluding professional affiliations from your resume. On the other hand, if there is sufficient space and the list of affiliations is both impressive and in some way related to your targeted position, I recommend you include them on the resume under the heading, Professional Affiliations. This section should be positioned to follow Experience, Military Service, or Patents and Publications, depending upon which of these categories was the last one listed on the resume.

If you have held a leadership position in these organizations, it is suggested (assuming there is sufficient space on the resume), that this information be spotlighted. The following is an example of how this might be done:

PROFESSIONAL
AFFILIATIONS: 1968–Pres.   Employment Management Assoc.
                                President   (1986–1987)
                                Vice President   (1985–1986)
                                Secretary   (1984–1985)

                 1980–1986   Amer. Soc. Personnel Admin.
                                Vice President   (1982–1983)

                 1978–1980   Phila. Personnel Association

COMMUNITY SERVICE

Unless you are applying for a position where community service is directly related to your job objective, or where it can demonstrate leadership (e.g., you have been chairperson, president, or vice president) it is recommended that this section not be included in the employment resume. Perhaps the only other exception to this is where it is known in advance that a specific employer is an advocate of community service, and strongly encourages its employees to get involved. In this case, there could be some reason to include this section in the resume.

Should you include community activities in your resume, it is suggested that a format similar to that for professional associations be used.

HOBBIES/ACTIVITIES

For the experienced person, the inclusion of hobbies and extracurricular activities adds little value to the resume unless, of course, these hobbies and activities are directly related to your qualifications for the position you seek. Generally, however, there is little, if any, relevance and these items are best left off the resume. Resume space could, in all likelihood, be better used to describe other aspects of your background that speak more directly to your skills and qualifications for the position you are seeking.

There are some who would argue that hobbies and activities should be included since they can show that you are someone with broad, diverse interests. There is no absolute recommendation that can be made here, and it is best to temper your decision with common sense. If there is sufficient space, and your hobbies are varied and interesting, you may wish to include this category on your resume. But, if you are short of space, or your list of hobbies and activities is small and lacks diversity, it might be best to exclude this information completely.

If you include a Hobbies/Activities section, position it as the last section of your resume. The generally accepted practice is to simply list hobbies and activities in the following manner:

HOBBIES/ACTIVITIES: Creative writing, antique restoration, skiing, skydiving, chess, and classical music.

Should any of these hobbies and activities suggest knowledge or skills that may be helpful to your employment candidacy, be sure to list these items first.

This ends the discussion of the chronological resume. If you have followed along, preparing each section, step-by-step, you should now have a complete and effective employment resume. The rest of this chapter consists of a number of sample chronological resumes for your review and reference.

Chronological Resume — Accounting

ARTHUR J. WARRINGTON
1325 North Lake Road
Chicago, IL 19743

Phone: (516) 875-2861

OBJECTIVE:

Senior level accounting position as Corporate or Division Controller.

EDUCATION:

M.B.A., Pennsylvania State University, 1983
Major: Financial Management
Grade Point Average: 3.7/4.0

B.A., Pennsylvania State University, 1981
Major: Accounting
Grade Point Average: 3.85/4.0

PROFESSIONAL CERTIFICATION:

C.P.A., Pennsylvania, 1987

EXPERIENCE:

1992
to
Pres.

NATIONAL BOTTLING COMPANY (CHICAGO, ILLINOIS)

Division Accounting Manager
Report to Division Manager of this $390 million beverage bottling and distribution division (5 plants, $105 million assets). Manage staff of 33 with full accounting and financial reporting accountability. Functional responsibility includes financial accounting, cost accounting, taxes, and payroll.

Achievements:

* Led successful installation and start-up of $2 million general ledger computer system resulting in 20% staff reduction and cutting financial reporting time by 50%. ($1.1 million annual savings).

* Converted to external service bureau for payroll processing ($1/4 million annual savings).

* Reclassified tax asset base yielding $120 thousand annual tax savings.

1987
to
1992

WALTER CHEMICALS, INC. (CORNING, NEW YORK)

Corporate Accounting Manager (1989-1992)
Reported to Director of Financial Accounting of this $225 million manufacturer of chemical specialties. Managed staff of 13 with functional responsibility for financial reporting, payroll, and taxes.

Chronological Resume —Accounting (Continued)

Achievements:

* Led implementation of "zero based budgeting" concept resulting in first year savings of $1.7 million.

* Directed successful installation and start-up of on-line computerized accounting system cutting 3 days off quarterly and annual closings.

* Reorganized Accounting Department with resultant 20% reduction in headcount ($200 annual savings).

Manager of Cost Accounting (1987-1989)
Reported to Corporate Accounting Manager. Managed staff of 3 with corporate-wide accountability for all cost accounting activities.

Achievement:

* Developed new cost accounting procedures to gain better financial control of raw materials inventory ($1.7 million annual cost savings).

1985 to 1987	**PEAT, MARWICK, MITCHELL & COMPANY (PHILADELPHIA, PA)**

Supervising Senior – Auditing   (1986-1987)
Staff Auditor   (1985-1986)

MILITARY SERVICE:

United States Marine Corps, 1983-1985
3rd Battalion, Airborne Division
Captain
Honorable Discharge, May 15, 1985

Chronological Resume —Engineering

MARK L. RILEY
Apartment 301
Arlington Towers
2235 Shively Blvd.
Baltimore, MD 17374

Phone: (301) 673-1863

OBJECTIVE:

Senior Project Engineer with stable, growing company offering opportunity for future advancement and professional growth.

EDUCATION:

M.S., University of Maryland, 1990
Major: Electrical Engineering
Grade Point Average: 3.6/4.0
Bolding Fellowship

B.S., University of Wisconsin, 1988
Major: Electrical Engineering
Grade Point Average: 3.8/4.0
Cum Laude Graduate

EXPERIENCE:

1990
to
Pres.

DELCO ELECTRONICS, INC.. (CORPORATE ENGINEERING)

Senior Project Engineer   (1993 to Present)
Report to Engineering Manager - Systems of this $775 million manufacturer of chemical control systems for papermaking wet-end applications. Engineer, install, start-up and debug complete computer control systems at customer sites in support of field sales organization. Provide on-call technical support to 13 existing customer sites and manage 3 to 5 new installations annually.

Achievements:

* Completed all projects on time, with most at or below budget ($1/2 million savings in 2 years).

* Introduced new System 2000 interface design resulting in 25% reduction in system installation costs ($2 million potential annual savings).

* Recipient of "Engineer of the Year" award (1993 & 1994).

Project Engineer   (1990-1993)
Reported to Senior Project Engineer. Provided engineering support in the design, installation, and start-up of System 2000 control system used for automated chemical control in papermaking processes.

Chronological Resume — Finance

WHITNEY R. MURRAY
1825 Broadmeadow Blvd.
Wyomissing Hills, PA 19635

Phone: (215) 472-8953

OBJECTIVE:

Chief Financial Officer with major corporation.

EXPERIENCE:

1989
to
Pres.

EARTHSTAR INTERNATIONAL CORP. (CORPORATE OFFICES)

Senior Vice President & Chief Financial Officer (1992 to Present)
Report to Executive Vice President - Administration of this $5 billion , Fortune 150 manufacturer of military aircraft and satellite equipment. Direct staff of 35 professionals with responsibility for all short and long-term financing to meet the present and future capital requirements of the business ($500 to $600 million annual capital requirements, $3.9 billion long-term debt portfolio). Functional responsibilities include: corporate finance, international finance, money & banking, credit, risk management, and pension funding.

Achievements:

* Refinanced total long-term debt load at substantially improved terms ($13 million million annual savings).

* Improved credit rating from AA to AAA, despite 25% increase in domestic debt load.

* Orchestrated aggressive investor relations program with resultant increase in stock price from $28 to $56 per common share.

Director of Financial Planning (1989-1992)
Reported to Vice President & Chief Financial Officer. Directed staff of 7 Financial Analysts with full responsibility for forecasting and planning the short and long-term capital requirements of the business ($550 to $600 million per year).

Achievements:

* Developed five-year financial planning computer model allowing substantially improved accuracy in forecasting capital requirements of international affiliates (22 companies, 18 countries).

* Directed restructuring of intermediate debt resulting in estimated annual savings of $9.5 million.

Chronological Resume —Finance (Continued)

1984
to
1989

WOLVINGTON ELECTRONICS, INC. (CORPORATE OFFICES)

Senior Analyst, Corporate Finance (1987-1989)
Reported to Director of Corporate Finance. Responsible for analyzing and recommending financing methods and sources for wide range of domestic and international clients. Provided consultation to top management of 3 business groups in the development of improved long-range capital plans and forecasts.

Achievements:

* Developed first believable financial forecasting model for management use on IBM PC.

* Provided complete financial analysis and recommendations on 6 potential acquisition targets.

Financial Analyst – Corporate Finance (1984-1987)
Reported to Senior Financial Analyst with responsibility to assist in the identification, analysis, and recommendation of a wide range of business opportunities and financing options.

EDUCATION:

M.B.A., Syracuse University, 1984
Major: Financial Planning

B.A., Bucknell University, 1982
Major: Accounting
Grade Point Average: 3.7/4.0
Dean's List, 1978-1982
Tarmac Scholarship, 1978-1982

Chronological Resume—Human Resources

MARY LYNN SEIGEL
Apartment 315
Cross Creek Apartments
Warfield, CT 18746

Phone: (513) 876-2948

OBJECTIVE:

Senior level management position with full responsibility for the corporate staffing and employment function.

EXPERIENCE:

1993
to
Pres.

WORTHINGTON ASSOCIATES, LTD. (NEW YORK, NY)

Vice President & Senior Consultant
Report to Executive Vice President of this major international executive search consulting firm (8 domestic offices, 22 overseas). Responsible for development of new clients and generation of revenue for the business by providing full range of executive search consulting services to client organizations in the staffing of middle and senior management level positions.

Achievements:

* Developed 9 new clients in first year, generating annual revenue of $215,000.

* Developed 11 new clients in second year, increasing annual revenue to $320,000 (a 49% increase).

* Improved the percentage of senior level searches from 25% to 40% of total assignments.

* Established strong rapport with existing client base, resulting in repeat business and several new business referrals.

1979
to
1993

CARLSON ELECTRONICS, INC. (WASHINGTON, DC)

Manager of Technical Employment (1989-1993)
Reported to Director of Corporate Employment for this 20,000 employee, Fortune 200 manufacturer of printed circuit boards and electronic components (annual sales $3.9 billion). Managed recruitment and employment of all technical and operations personnel for corporate staff, 4 profit centers, and 20 manufacturing facilities.

Achievements:

* Successfully staffed $1.5 billion capital expansion program - hiring 265 engineers 18 technical & operations managers, and 7 senior staff members (director and vice president level)

* Reduced interview-to-offer ratio from 8:1 to 2:1 - a 400% improvement ($1.5 million estimated savings).

* Reduced offer-to-hire ratio from 3:1 to 1.5:1 - a 200% improvement.

Chronological Resume —Human Resources (Continued)

Manager of Human Resources & Employment Services (1985-1989)
Reported to Director of Human Resources of this 1,200 employee, high technology division engaged in the precision coating of photographic film and the manufacture & development of photoimaging equipment. Responsibilities included human resource planning, organization design, employment & staffing, training & development, salary & benefits administration, and human relations management.

Achievements:

* Served as lead human resources consultant to top management in the planning, design, staffing, and successful start-up of new TEP business unit.

* Led employee turnover study that resulted in action plan which reduced turnover among technical professionals from 15% to less than 3% per year (annual savings of $2.4 million).

Plant Personnel Manager (1982-1985)
Reported to Plant Manager with the responsibility for the development and implementation of plant human resources programs, policies, and procedures for this 250 employee, non-union printed circuit manufacturing facility. Managed staff of 3 with functional accountability for employee relations, staffing & employment, wage & salary administration, training, benefits, medical, safety & security, communications, and public relations.

Personnel Assistant (1979-1982)
Entry level human resources position in 2,500 employee electronic components manufacturing plant.

EDUCATION:

B.A., Bucknell University, 1979
Major: Business Administration

PROFESSIONAL AFFILIATIONS:

1984-Pres.	Employment Management Association	
	President	(1994)
	Vice President	(1993)
	Secretary	(1992)

1989-1994	National Association of Corporate & Professional Recruiters
1981-1994	Society for Human Resources Management
1989-1994	Human Resources Planning Society

Chronological Resume —Marketing & Sales

KATHERINE A LARSON
875 Wallace Street
Troy, MI 18735

Phone: (513) 374-8926

OBJECTIVE:

Senior level corporate position in marketing & sales management.

EXPERIENCE:

1992
to
Pres.

BRITANNY EQUIPMENT COMPANY, INC. (CORPORATE OFFICES)

Vice President of Marketing & Sales (1995-Present)
Report to President of this Fortune 300, $1.9 billion manufacturer of earth moving, excavation, and mining equipment. Direct 125 employee marketing and sales organization ($115 million annual budget) with functional responsibility for market research & planning, market development, advertising & promotion, and field sales.

Achievements:

* Revamped sales compensation and training programs resulting in 25% increase in sales ($380 million) in less than 2 years.

* Reduced headcount by 10% through redesign of sales districts (($3/4 million annual savings).

* Led successful introduction of new Huffy bulldozer line selling 15 units in only 6 months (during declining market).

Director of Marketing & Sales (1992-1995)
Reported to Vice President of Marketing & Sales with functional responsibility for all marketing and sales functions (150 employees, $105 million budget).

Achievements:

* Led development of nation-wide dealership network (25 cities) to sell new Big Kat line to major highway contractors achieving major market share penetration (32%) in only 3 years.

* Tripled sales of Mighty Mack miniature dozer line ($25 to $75 million) in 2 years through product modification and repositioning of product to target the residential developer market segment.

1888
to
1992

BULL DOG TRUCKS, INC. (WARREN, OHIO)

National Sales Manager
Reported to Vice President of Marketing of this $765 million manufacturer of light duty dump trucks sold to light commercial and residential developer markets. Managed 65 employee field sales organization covering 30 states ($7.3 million budget).

Chronological Resume —Marketing & Sales (Continued)

Achievements:

* Realized 26% sales increase in 2 years through major restructuring of field sales organization.

* Initiated new sales strategy and bonus plan that increased market share of Little Bull product line by 25% in 3 years.

* Increased Big Bull market share by 18% during same period.

1982
to
1988

ROTHCHILD EQUIPMENT COMPANY (ERIE, PA)

Senior Sales Representative (1985-1988)
Reported to Sales Manager of this $85 million regional marketer and distributor of street cleaning equipment. Sold street cleaning equipment to municipalities in three state area (Pennsylvania, New York and Virginia).

Achievements:

* Increased territory sales by 300% in 3 years.

* Named "Salesperson of the Year" (1986,1987, & 1988)

Sales Representative (1982-1985)
Reported to Sales Manager. Sold street cleaning equipment to municipalities in eastern Pennsylvania and New York State.

EDUCATION:

B.A., Pennsylvania State University, 1982
Major: Business Administration
Varsity Field Hockey, 1979-1982
Varsity Field Hockey Captain, 1981 & 1982

Chronological Resume —Materials Management

MARGARET R. TEMPLE
815 General Howe Drive
East Chester, PA 19385

Phone: (215) 420-7836

OBJECTIVE:

Corporate vice president in materials and logistics management.

EDUCATION:

M.B.A., Harvard Business School, 1983
Major: Finance

B.S., Princeton University, 1981
Major: Industrial Engineering
Grade Point Average: 3.8/4.0
Ford Motor Scholarship, 1977-1981
General Foods Scholarship, 1980

EXPERIENCE:

1993
to
Pres.

AMERICAN OIL COMPANY (HOUSTON, TEXAS)

Director of Transportation
Report to Vice President of Distribution of this $8 billion exploration and production company. Direct multinational staff of 285 transportation professionals ($200 million budget) in the international transport of $1.9 billion crude and refined product annually. Negotiate and administer large volume contracts for air & ocean transportation, trucking, heavy lift movement, container leasing & repair, import/export, cargo documentation, and customs brokerage. Senior advisor to Corporate Management on all international transportation matters.

Achievements:

* Reduced transportation costs by 10% ($20 million savings) in two years through implementation of computerized transportation planning and scheduling system.

* Cut transportation delivery time by 15% through improved loading techniques and better transport scheduling system.

1988
to
1993

VECTOR FOUNDRY COMPANY (PITTSBURGH, PA)

Director of Materials Management
Reported to Vice President Operations of this $180 million iron foundry. Managed staff of 65 with functional responsibility for purchasing ($100 million), traffic, stores, and raw materials control.

Chronological Resume —Materials Management (Continued)

Achievements:

* Led raw materials cost reduction initiatives resulting in $3 million annual savings.

* Installed raw materials planning and scheduling computer system saving $1/2 million annually.

1983
to
1988

BELLVILLE FOUNDRY, INC. (BELLVILLE, OHIO)

Manager of Operations Planning & Analysis (1986-1988)
Reported to Director of Operations. Analyzed company operations, prepared business plans and corporate reports for senior management. Coordinated capital expenditure, energy conservation, government price control reporting, and cost reduction programs.

Manager of Production Planning (1983-1986)
Reported to Operations Manager with responsibility for forecasting, production planning & scheduling, and inventory control systems.

Chronological Resume —Operations

JEFFREY A. MORSE
125 East Lansing Street
Lansing, MI 17465

Phone: (318) 763-2959 - Work
(318) 763-3887 - Office

OBJECTIVE:

Senior level operations management position with corporate-wide accountability.

EXPERIENCE:

1990
to
Pres.

ENVIRO–SCIENCE COMPANY, INC. (CORPORATE OFFICES)

Vice President of Operations (1995-Present)
Report to President of this $575 million manufacturer of air and water pollution control equipment. Direct the activities of 6 person corporate Operations staff and 5 plant manufacturing facilities employing 6,300 employees ($400 million budget).

Achievements:

* Directed corporate-wide implementation of SPC-based "total quality" effort resulting in 20% scrap reduction in 2 years ($80 million annual savings).

* Led creation of "Customer First" program reducing customer complaints by 85% in 2 years.

* Directed implementation of "high performance work system" concepts at 2 manufacturing sites resulting in increased employee participation and a 10% improvement in manufacturing productivity ($15 million annual savings).

* Implemented corporate-wide JIT inventory management program resulting in 18% reduction in raw materials inventories ($7.3 million annual savings).

Plant Manager – Wakefield Plant (1990-1995)
Reported to Vice President of Operations with P&L responsibility for this 1,600 employee fume incinerator manufacturing plant ($130 million annual production). Functions managed include manufacturing, distribution, engineering & maintenance, procurement, accounting, and human resources.

Achievements:

* Directed joint union/management cost reduction task force which implemented programs resulting in $11 million annual savings.

* Led successful start-up of metal fabrication assembly line beating learning curve by 4 months and start-up budget by 14% ($3 million first year savings).

* Recipient of "Plant of the Year" award (1993, 1994 & 1995).

Chronological Resume —Operations (Continued)

1983 to 1990	**BORK AIR CONDITIONING, INC. (CORPORATE OFFICES)**

Manager of Corporate Engineering (1985-1990)
Reported to Vice President of Manufacturing of this $260 million manufacturer of commercial and industrial air conditioners. Managed 85 employee corporate engineering department with responsibility for engineering design, installation, and start-up of metal fabrication and air conditioner assembly facilities.

Achievements:

* Directed successful engineering and start-up of $500 million worth of capital projects over 5 year period.

* Led successful engineering and start-up of $320 million fabrication and assembly facility - completed on time and $1.6 million under budget.

Department Manager – Fabrication (1983-1985)
Managed 120 employee Tampa Plant metal cabinet fabrication department with annual production value of $85 million.

Achievement:

* Changed line layout resulting in 13% productivity increase ($9 million annual savings).

EDUCATION:

B.S., University of Michigan, 1983
Major: Mechanical Engineering
Grade Point Average: 3.6/4.0
General Motors Scholarship (4 years)

Chronological Resume —Information Services

LINDA D. BAKER
202 Fairview Avenue
Atlanta, GA 87264

Phone: (414) 326-1987

OBJECTIVE:

Senior corporate level management position in information services.

EXPERIENCE:

1994
to
Pres.

SOFTWORK SYSTEMS, INC. (CORPORATE OFFICES)

Vice President – Information Resources
Report to President of this $50 million software development and marketing company with functional accountability for strategic planning, product development, and marketing. Direct staff of 350 employees in the development and sale of specialized accounting and cost control software to hospitals throughout the United States and Canada.

Achievements:

* Developed new IDMS-based general ledger software product that captured 23% of the community hospital market in the Northeast Region.

* Led sales expansion into new Southern Region which now produces $18 million in annual sales revenue.

* Developed and implemented successful site-based operating methodologies that have greatly facilitated data conversion at customer sites.

1992
to
1994

MONTGOMERY COUNTY (NORRISTOWN, PA)

Director of Information Services
Reported to Director of Administration with responsibility for providing information services to County management, including all telecommunications (voice, data, video, and radio) and data processing services. Managed 225 employee staff and annual budget of $13 million.

Achievements:

* Led major reorganization resulting in 8% reduction in staff with simultaneous 10% productivity increase ($3/4 million annual savings).

* Successfully transitioned from traditional "top down" management system to a "participative management" approach to department leadership.

* Established on-site personal computer training center facilitating rapid spread of PC utilization and increased employee productivity.

Chronological Resume —Information Services (Continued)

1988
to
1992

COMPUWARE DATA CORPORATION (CORPORATE OFFICES)

General Manager – Peripheral Systems
Reported to Director of Marketing with responsibility for developing market strategy for introduction of plug-compatible peripherals to IBM marketplace outside the United States. Directed 18 country, 22 employee international marketing organization with accountability for development and implementation of overall marketing and sales strategy.

Achievements:

* Generated annual sales of $38 million and profits of $9 million in 2 years from date of initial market entry.

* Initiative successful reliability testing process to ensure proper quality control of products prior to international shipment.

1986
to
1988

PIMA COUNTY (TUCSON, AZ)

Director of Data Processing
Reported to Vice President of Administration. Directed 40 person staff ($1.2 million annual budget) providing data processing services to all County departments.

Achievement:

* Used "participatory management" concepts to substantially improve morale and productivity of Data Processing Department.

1980
to
1986

DARLINGTON CORPORATION (CORPORATE OFFICES)

Senior Systems Analyst (1984-1986)
Reported to MIS Manager with responsibility for installation and start-up of $2 million general ledger accounting system.

Systems Analyst (1980-1984)
Evaluated and recommended several software packages for various client applications.

EDUCATION:

M.S., University of Virginia, 1980
Major: Computer Science
Grade Point Average: 3.6/4.0

8

Writing the Functional Resume

The functional resume format has long been one of the more popular resume formats. Second only to the chronological format in popularity, the functional resume is the second most widely used resume style, representing about 20 to 25 percent of all resumes received by employers. It deserves some thoughtful consideration when deciding what resume style will best present your credentials to a prospective employer.

As discussed in Chapter 6, Resume Style—Picking the Right One, there are times when use of the functional resume is clearly not in your best interest. If you have not already done so, it would behoove you to read Chapter 6 before arbitrarily choosing the functional format. In most instances, in fact, you will find that chronological resume format will better serve your needs.

Before you elect to use the functional resume, you need to be aware that the single greatest drawback to use of this format is that it is the style most frequently used when the employment candidate has something to hide. Typically, it is used to disguise such things as:

1. Lack of career progress

2. Lack of career continuity

3. Frequent changes of job/employer

4. Periods of lengthy or frequent unemployment

5. Lack of prerequisite experience for position

6. Lack of prerequisite education for position

7. Age.

Seasoned employment professionals are immediately suspicious when they see a functional resume. Instead of focusing on the candidate's credentials, therefore, there is a tendency to try to find out what the candidate is attempting to conceal. This sets up some negative thoughts right from the start, which may cause the employer to shy away from your candidacy.

Rather than discourage your use of the functional resume entirely, it is important to point out that there are certain times when the functional resume is, in fact, the preferred resume format. Chapter 6 provides excellent guidelines for making this determination, and should be read carefully before choosing which format you will use. After all, you want the best format working for you that you can get—the one that most effectively markets you and your background to prospective employers. Don't leave resume format selection to chance, it's simply too important to your job hunting campaign.

OVERVIEW OF FUNCTIONAL FORMAT

The functional resume, (unlike the chronological resume, which focuses on the chronology of positions held), focuses on the employment candidate's background and accomplishments under broad functional categories. When using this resume style, the author will want to choose those functional areas most related to the position sought, and then to cite specific experience and accomplishments related to each of these key functional categories. Functional categories chosen for highlighting are normally those thought to be important functional accountabilities of the position for which the job candidate is applying.

By choosing functional areas important to the target job, and citing evidence of your ability to achieve meaningful results in these areas, it is believed that the functional resume format can be a fairly powerful tool. If well-prepared, such a presentation can showcase historical evidence of your overall qualifications and capabilities and will certainly get the employer's attention.

This same approach can be used to focus on job-related skills as well. This is known as "skills-based" functional resume. In this case, you simply select specific skills that are important to job performance and emphasize these skill areas instead of job functions. As with the function-based resume, under each skill heading you cite examples of specific results and accomplishments which demonstrate proficiency in these key skill areas. The skill-based resume format is most frequently used by candidates having little or no functional experience in the areas required by the position. Typically, this approach is used by recent graduates or persons having little or no job-related experience.

The key advantage of the functional resume is that it permits the employment candidate to focus on key job functions or job skills and to draw the employer's attention to his or her strengths in these important areas. The remainder of this chapter will be devoted to leading you through a step-by-step process for preparing an effective functional resume.

RESUME COMPONENTS

Review of the sample functional resumes at the end of this chapter will reveal that the functional resume has five basic components:

1. Heading

2. Summary

3. Major accomplishments

4. Work History

5. Education.

Unlike the chronological resume, the order in which these components are presented on the resume does not vary. Instead, they are listed in the same order as they appear here. The reason for this is fairly logical. The emphasis of this resume format is on functional accomplishments and these must therefore be presented at the beginning of the resume. To list education or work history before major accomplishments would take the focus away from these accomplishments and would, therefore, be self-defeating.

Beyond these basic components, as with the chronological resume, there are some optional components which you may or may not wish to include. They are:

1. Professional certification

2. Professional affiliations

3. Publications

4. Patents

5. Community service

6. Hobbies/activities.

For a thorough discussion of these optional areas, refer back to Chapter 7. The focus here will be on how to prepare the basic components of the functional resume.

What follows is a detailed review of each basic component of the functional resume. By following the step-by-step instructions provided here, you will end up with a well-prepared and effective functional resume.

HEADING

Preparation of the resume heading is simple and straightforward. Essentially, there are three elements to the resume heading. They are:

1. Name

2. Address

3. Telephone number.

Review of the sample resumes at the end of this chapter will reveal that all three parts of the heading are centered. In addition, there are three spaces separating the resume heading from the rest of the text. You will also note that the candidate's name is printed in capital letters and bold type, causing it to stand out from the rest of the heading

Although it is common practice to list home phone number in the resume heading, there has long been a debate by resume professionals whether the work phone number should also be included. Listing the work number may raise some questions on the part of prospective employers concerning why you will allow contact at your place of employment. Perhaps you have already been terminated by your current employer and are being allowed to conduct your job search from your employer's office? Perhaps you are expecting to be terminated shortly and really don't care if your employer discovers that you are looking for other employment? Perhaps you are a person who frequently uses company time to conduct personal business? These and other similar questions may enter the prospective employer's mind if you include your office phone number in the resume heading. None of these reflects favorably on your employment candidacy.

Generally, it is recommended that the work phone number be excluded from the employment resume. Prospective employers, who want to reach you can use the mail or can send a wire to your home address. In addition, they can call you at home during evening hours (a very common practice among employment professionals). If you are difficult to reach by phone, you might consider using the cover letter, which accompanies your resume, to list the name and phone number of a trusted individual who can normally be reached during working hours, and who can relay a message to you.

Further review of the sample resumes contained in this chapter will show that the telephone number is separated from the rest of the heading by use of double spacing. This provides for ease of reading and fast location in the event the employer wishes to contact you.

SUMMARY

The intended purpose of the resume's summary section is to give the employer just enough information about you to compel reading of the balance of your resume. This is normally done by conveying some idea of the depth and breadth of your experience and by also highlighting some of your key strengths in areas of likely interest to the prospective employer.

Review of the sample resumes at the end of this chapter will reveal that summary sections have some similarities. First, the initial sentence of each summary statement reports the writer's career or professional area, and cites the number of years of experience. The second sentence is normally used to market key job-related strengths. Finally, the third sentence is normally used to further convey the breadth of the candidate's experience. Alternately, this third sentence can be used to further market some unique skill or fact that would likely be perceived as valuable by the prospective employer.

The summary section of the resume should be concise and to-the-point. It should not be a lengthy, rambling epistle.

Component statements need not be written in complete sentences. Instead, they may be written as simple descriptive phrases that are intended to be hard-hitting and concise—much the same as the approach used in advertising. One simple rule to be used in accomplishing this is to begin each statement with an adjective followed by a noun. This will force you to be brief and to the point.

MAJOR ACCOMPLISHMENTS

When organizing this section of the resume, it is best to start by mentally focusing on the target job you are seeking, and then asking yourself the following questions:

1. What are the key functional responsibilities of the target position?

2. How should these be ranked in order of their importance to the position?

3. In which of these functional areas do I have meaningful experience?

4. What have been my three or four major accomplishments in each of these functional areas?

Considerable time can be saved at this point by referring to the preliminary work already done by you in Chapter 5. By referring back to this chapter, it should be relatively easy for you to quickly identify your major accomplishments. Although they are arranged in chronological job sequence, it should be simple to classify them under the functional categories that you have chosen to highlight on your resume.

If you have little or no relevant experience, as an alternate to this functions-based approach, you may wish to use the skills-based approach to the functional resume. Should you elect to do this, you will need to answer the following questions:

1. What is the position I am seeking?

2. What are the key functional accountabilities of this target position?

3. What are the key skills necessary to successful performance of these functions?

4. Which of these skills have I acquired?

5. How have I used these skills and with what results?

In this case, instead of highlighting functional areas on the resume, you will want to choose broad skill categories that are important to functional job performance. Under each of these broad skill categories, you should list major accomplishments or results that demonstrate your skill proficiency in each of these relevant skill areas.

When listing the functional or skill areas you wish to stress on your resume, it is important that these categories be presented in order of priority. Those categories considered to be most important to the target position should be listed first, with least relevant category listed last.

Although this sequence is the most frequently recommended to functional resume writers, there are times when the ordering of these categories should be based upon criteria other than just job-relatedness. In particular, where some of your accomplishments and results under one of these categories are clearly outstanding when compared to other functional or skill categories, such category should be listed first on the resume with the others assuming a subordinate role. The logic that supports this sequencing is the old adage, *Lead with your strength.* All else being equal, however, it is best to arrange these categories in accordance with their importance to the target position, as suggested in the previous paragraph.

Review of the sample resumes contained in this chapter will show that each of the category headings chosen for emphasis should be underlined with the first letter of each word in caps.

Additionally, to improve resume aesthetics and overall readability, each category heading should be preceded and followed by double spacing.

In keeping with the power writing principles outlined in Chapter 5, each of the accomplishment statements listed under the functional categories should be started with a verb. This will force you to write brief, meaningful statements. Where possible, such result statements should contain quantitative information which provides the reader with some understanding of the magnitude of the result. This is particularly true if such results were of significant magnitude (e.g., a 40 percent increase in sales, a 25 percent reduction in costs, a 60 percent increase in productivity, etc.).

As with the functional (or skill) categories themselves, the statements of accomplishment listed under each of these categories should be listed in order of their importance to the overall functional accountability of the target position. Here again, where a particular accomplishment has significantly more impact than others (included under the same functional category), such accomplishment should be listed first, with the balance of results statements following. Once again, *Lead with your strength!*

WORK HISTORY

The work history section of the resume should be organized in reverse chronological order. Start first with your current or most recent employer, and then go backwards in time to the first employer for whom you worked. The format followed here is similar to that used in the chronological resume with the exception that no descriptions of positions are provided.

Review of the sample resumes at the end of this chapter will show the following consistent sequence:

1. Dates of employment with each individual employer are listed at the left hand margin.

2. Names and locations of the employers are then listed to the right of these employment dates. Both the name of the employer and location are underlined with the first letter in each word in both the employer's name and location printed in caps. (This provides for ease of readership.)

3. The title of each position held with a respective employer is then listed in reverse chronological order (i.e., most recent position held listed first). The first letter of each word in the job tile is capitalized.

4. The dates of employment for each position held are listed in brackets to the right of the position. (This serves to avoid confusion concerning which positions were held with which employer and makes it perfectly clear that these dates are job-related.)

5. Note the use of spacing. Double spacing is used to separate employers, with single spacing used between titles of positions held. (This serves to visually separate employers, thus providing for ease of reading.)

EDUCATION

As with the chronological resume, the education section of the functional resume should include the following information in the sequence shown:

1. Line 1: Degree awarded, school, and date of graduation

2. Line 2: Major (and minor, if applicable)

3. Line 3: Grade point average (List if 3.0/4.0) or higher; exclude if less than 3.0/4.0

4. Line 4: Class rank (List if top 10%; exclude if lower than top 10%)

5. Line 5: Scholarships/fellowships and years awarded

6. Line 6: Honors/awards and years awarded

Although Education is generally positioned to follow the Work History section, it can be listed first if to do so would strengthen the overall impact of the resume. The questions you need to ask is, "Which category—Education or Work History—contains the most job-related and impressive credentials?" For the experienced person, the answer will most likely be Work History. For the person with little or no work experience, however, the answer could well be Education. When in doubt, the rule of thumb is to position Work History before Education. This is a functional resume, after all, and the whole purpose is to draw attention to your functional credentials for the target position. This is usually defeated when Work History is positioned after Education.

The balance of this chapter provides you with some sample functional resume for your review and reference.

Functional Resume

ARTHUR J. WARRINGTON
1325 North Lake Road
Chicago, IL 19743

Phone: (516) 875-2861

SUMMARY:

Seasoned accounting manager with 11 years experience in business and public accounting. Broad general accounting experience at the corporate, division, and manufacturing levels. Strong record of cost control and savings contributions.

MAJOR ACCOMPLISHMENTS:

Corporate Accounting

- Directed corporate accounting function for $225 million specialty chemicals manufacturer.

- Managed staff of 13 with functional accountability for financial reporting, accounting, payroll, and taxes.

- Installed on-line computer accounting system cutting 3 days off quarterly and year-end closings.

- Reduced department by 25% through reorganization.

- Installed "zero-based" budgeting program resulting in $1.7 million annual savings.

Division Accounting

- Directed division accounting function for $390 million bottling operation (5 franchises, $150 million assets).

- Managed staff of 33 with functional accountability for financial reporting, cost accounting, tax, and payroll.

- Implemented new computerized general ledger system.

- Converted to external service bureau payroll processing ($1/4 million annual savings).

- Reclassified tax asset base ($120 thousand annual tax savings).

Functional Resume (Continued)

Cost Accounting

- Managed corporate cost accounting department (staff of 3).

- Installed inventory cost control system ($1.7 million savings).

- Implemented new manufacturing cost standards resulting in identification of major source of energy wastage (($3/4 million annual savings).

WORK HISTORY:

1993 to Pres.	**National Bottling Company (Chicago, IL)** Division Accounting Manager	
1988 to 1993	**Walter Chemicals, Inc. (Corning, NY)** Corporate Accounting Manager Manager of Cost Accounting	(1990-1993) (1988-1990)
1986 to 1988	**Peat, Marwick, Mitchell & Company (Philadelphia, PA)** Supervising Senior - Auditing Staff Auditor	(1987-1988) (1986-1987)

EDUCATION:

M.B.A., Pennsylvania State University, 1986
Major: Financial Management
Grade Point Average: 3.7/4.0

B.A., Pennsylvania State University, 1984
Major: Accounting
Grade Point Average: 3.85/4.0
Alcoa Scholarship,   1982-1984
Lassiter Scholarship, 1981-1982

PROFESSIONAL CERTIFICATION:

C.P.A., Commonwealth of Pennsylvania, May 1988

Functional Resume

MARY LYNN SEIGEL
Apartment 315
Cross Creek Apartments
825 Cross Creek Road
Warfield, CT 18746

Phone: (513) 876-2948

SUMMARY:

Human resources professional with 17 years experience in manufacturing and consulting. Strong background in executive search, employment, staffing, and human resources generalist areas.

MAJOR ACCOMPLISHMENTS:

Executive Search

- Senior consultant with major international executive search firm (4 years).

- Successfully completed numerous assignments at various organizational levels (president, vice president, director, and middle management).

- Generated $230,000 annual revenue in second year (50% increase).

- Generated $350,000 annual revenue in third year (52% increase).

Employment

- Technical Employment Manager for Fortune 200 company (4 years).

- Provided employment support to 4 profit centers (20 plants, 18,000 employees).

- Successfully staffed $1.5 billion capital expansion and modernization program.

- Recruited and hired 265 engineers, 18 managers, and 7 division officers in 1 year.

- Achieved 2:1 interview-to-hire ratio (400% improvement) in 3 years.

- Achieved 1.5:1 offer-to-hire ratio (200% improvement) in 3 years.

Human Resources Generalist

- Managed Human Resources and Employment Services Department for 1,200 employee high technology division.

- Managed Human Resources Department for 250 employee, non-union manufacturing plant.

Functional Resume (Continued)

<u>**WORK HISTORY**</u>:

1994 to Pres.	<u>**Worthington Associates, Ltd (New York, NY)**</u> Senior Consultant	

1980 to 1994	<u>**Carlson Electronics, Inc. (Washington, DC)**</u>	
	Manager of Technical Employment	(1990-1994)
	Manager of H.R. & Employment Services	(1986-1990)
	Plant Human Resources Manager	(1983-1986)
	Human Resources Assistant	(1980-1983)

<u>**EDUCATION**</u>:

B.A., Bucknell University, 1980
Major: Business Administration

<u>**PROFESSIONAL AFFILIATIONS**</u>:

Employment Management Association		1985-Present
President	(1996)	
Vice President	(1995)	
Secretary	(1994)	
National Association of Corp. & Professional Recruiters		1990-1996
Society for Human Resources Management		1990-1997
Human Resources Planning Society		1992-1997

9

Key Employment Sources and How to Use Them

When beginning your employment search, it is important to realize that there are a number of sources that can be used to help you to find the position you are seeking. You should think creatively about the various sources that are at your disposal and how to best use them to your advantage.

Most people, when asked to list sources of jobs, will list only a relatively small number. These typically include:

Newspaper ads

Employment agencies

Executive search firms

State employment services

Actually, there are many more employment sources that can effectively be used to assist you in your job search. The purpose of this chapter is to introduce you to several of these sources and suggest ways in which they might be effectively used to help you achieve your job search objectives.

LOCAL NEWSPAPERS

The classified section of your local newspaper is perhaps the best known source of job opportunities. This does not mean, however, that it is the most productive. Knowledgeable sources estimate that only between 10 and 14 percent of all jobs filled in the United States are filled as a result of newspaper advertising. This is a fairly small percentage considering the importance attached to this source by most inexperienced job hunters. You should certainly not depend upon this as the major employment source when planning your job search campaign.

When using the local newspaper as a source in your job hunting campaign, it is important to think creatively about its use. Here are some guidelines that will help you get the most out of your newspapers:

1. Read the classified ads for specific positions that are of interest to you, and respond by sending a copy of your resume along with appropriate cover letter.

2. Read the business section. Look for firms that are expanding in some way (e.g., constructing new buildings, introducing new products, installing new equipment, opening new markets, acquiring other companies). Also, look for signs of solid economic health (record sales and profits). Healthy, expanding firms are usually hiring and should be included among your target firms for contact. Don't ignore firms that are experiencing difficulty—especially if you have the skills and capability to assist them in solving their problems.

3. Carefully read announcements of internal promotions as well as new appointments from sources outside of the

company. Generally speaking, when someone is promoted there is normally need for a replacement. Likewise, in the case of external employment, the past employer will also have a spot to fill.

4. The obituary column can also be a source of job leads. If the deceased is not of retirement age, it is not uncommon for the newspaper article to list current employer and position held. In many cases, the employer will need to hire someone to fill the job vacancy.

SPECIALTY NEWSPAPERS

There are certain specialty newspapers that are geared specifically to the job hunter. These papers are normally a composite of employment ads run in major newspapers throughout the country. Two of the most popular are:

The National Ad Search

This is a weekly tabloid that is a compilation of employment want ads from seventy-two key newspapers across the United States. Over 2,000 ads are clipped, indexed and arranged into 42 executive, professional and technical categories for quick, easy reference. This weekly tabloid can be ordered by contacting National Ad Search, Inc., P.O. Box 2083, Milwaukee, WI 53101 (Phone toll-free: 1-800-992-2832).

The National Business Employment Weekly

This is a weekly tabloid published by *The Wall Street Journal* and is readily available at most newsstands and drugstores. It is a compilation of all want ad advertising run in the regional editions of *The Wall Street Journal* during the past week.

Both of these specialty newspapers can serve as excellent supplements to your local newspaper, provided, of course, you are willing to relocate to other areas of the United States. Since many of these ads are already a week or so old when they are published in these specialty papers, it is important for you to respond quickly to any ad that is of interest to you.

PROFESSIONAL ASSOCIATIONS

An important source frequently overlooked by the job seeker is professional associations. Many of these associations provide various job hunting services free of charge to their members. Such services take many forms including:

1. Computer job banks for use by both employers and individual members (The association matches employer job listings with member resumes, and forwards appropriate resumes to employer.)

2. Free job opportunity listings provided to member companies in association newsletter

3. Free *Situations Wanted* section in association's newsletter, permitting individual members to advertise their availability and summary of qualifications

4. Association sponsored job fairs where members can sign up and interview with prospective employers

5. Coordination of job hunting service programs during local, regional, or national meetings (Such coordination ranges from announcements of career opportunities at meetings, to job opportunity bulletin boards, to arranging actual interview meetings between job seeking members and prospective employers.)

All that is usually required is a little research and a few phone calls to the association's national, regional, or local headquarters. Most associations are always looking to increase their membership and welcome the opportunity to explain their services to prospective new members.

If you are unsure about how to identify associations that are related to your professional career interests, I suggest that you visit your local library and do a little research using the *Encyclopedia of Associations*. This handy reference book lists thousands of non-profit American membership organizations of national scope, including professional societies, trade associations, labor unions, and the like. A key word index facilitates location of organizations associated with particular subjects.

TRADE/INDUSTRIAL ASSOCIATIONS

Trade or industrial associations can also prove worthwhile employment sources. As with professional associations, they frequently provide some sort of employment services to their membership. The types of services provided and methods for researching such associations are the same as with professional associations.

TRADE AND PROFESSIONAL PUBLICATIONS

Although many trade or professional associations produce their own publications, there are frequently well-read trade and professional publications that are independently published. Such publications, because of their particular focus on specific industries or professions, frequently become the targets for recruitment advertising that is specifically directed to persons having experience in these industries or occupational specialties.

Some well-spent time with the librarian in the periodical section of the library will quickly surface most of these key publications. The national officers of trade and professional associations are usually also very knowledgeable of these publications and will gladly furnish you with their names just for the asking.

EMPLOYMENT AGENCIES

There is generally a good deal of confusion among the general public concerning the difference between an employment agency and an executive search firm. Perhaps the following characteristics will help you to make the distinction:

Characteristics of Executive Search Firms

1. Hired, under contact, by employer to represent the employer's interests in identifying and recruiting candidates for a specific position

2. Legally, acts as the agent of the employer and is fully responsible to the client company for results of the search project

3. Works only on an exclusive basis (i.e., no other firm represents the employer and the employer is using no other sources to fill this position)

4. Is paid a predetermined consulting fee by the client company, regardless of the outcome of the search project (i.e., is compensated for consulting time)

5. Is reimbursed by the client company for all direct, out-of-pocket expenses incurred while conducting the search assignment

6. Always conducts a thorough, face-to-face interview with prospective candidates and prepares a complete candidate report prior to presenting candidate to client company

7. Always conducts thorough reference check and prepares complete written reference report on finalist candidates for submission to client company (Usually done prior to interview with client company)

8. Never represents job seekers in their search for employment opportunities

Characteristics of Employment Agencies

1. Generally represents the individual who is seeking employment, rather than the employer

2. May sometimes represent the employer, but there is never a binding consulting contract

3. Is never paid for consulting time—is only paid when, and if, assignment is successfully completed (i.e., position is filled)

4. Seldom has an exclusive on the assignment—must frequently compete with others to fill position

5. Is seldom, if ever, reimbursed by the employer for expenses incurred in carrying out assignment

6. Almost never conducts a face-to-face interview with candidate—unless candidate's own resume (rather than written report) as the basis for presentation to the employer

7. Seldom, if ever, checks candidate references—no reference report submitted to employer.

Employment agencies are sometimes referred to as *contingency* firms. This means that they receive no compensation unless they are successful in placing a candidate in the position. Because of this, employment agencies tend, as a group, to be considerably less objective than executive search firms. Because of the contingency nature of their operations there may be a much higher tendency to try to put a square peg in a round hole.

There are an estimated 8,000 to 10,000 employment agencies in the United States. Although there are some who do a thorough, professional job in representing employment candidates, unfortunately, there are a fair number who are simply out to make a buck, and have little concern for the interests of either the candidate or the employer. Their only concern is to quickly make a placement, collect their money, and move on to the next assignment. There are all too many of these type firms, and they have given the industry at large a very bad name. It can be difficult to know who the truly professional, reputable firms really are.

Although I would not entirely discourage use of employment agencies, I would recommend that you proceed cautiously and be sure that you are dealing with those who are ethical and professional in their dealings. In order to find out who these better firms are, I would suggest that, using your personal contacts, you secure the names of a half dozen or so employment managers from major corporations and contact them for their recommendations on the names of some of the better agencies who specialize in your field.

Since individual consultants within the same firm can vary considerably with respect to their professionalism and effectiveness, I suggest that you also secure endorsements on the names of the better consultants in each of these recommended firms. It is best to use the names of these employment managers when contacting the recommended consultants. Tell them that they were suggested by a particular employment manager. They will normally feel flattered by this and will likely make a special effort to assist you.

When time, distance, and cost permit, you should personally visit each of the firms with whom you will be dealing. Call in advance and make an appointment with the consultant who will be representing you. During your actual visit, make sure there is a thorough understanding of your background, qualifications, and job search objectives. Failure to do this could result in improper representation of your credentials and interests, and waste considerable time for both you and the prospective employers.

If employed at the time of your job search, you will want to be particularly careful to select firms who will not expose you to unnecessary risks. In particular, you will need to be assured that your resume will not be plastered all over the universe and that it will not be inadvertently sent to your current employer. To guard against this, you may want to control circulation of your resume by coming to some sort of agreement with the agency counselor concerning the specific circumstances under which your resume would be presented to a particular employer. Additionally, so there are no mistakes, you may also want to furnish this counselor with the names of all divisions, subsidiaries, and affiliate companies that are part of, or associated with, your current employer.

As an additional word of caution, when using employment agencies, many of these firms are members of large associations that share resumes and job listings with other associations' members. Some of the larger of these associations have several thousand member firms. If currently employed, mass circulation of your resume to association membership, with subsequent mailing by these member firms as part of a mass promotional mailing, may not exactly be in your best interests. I would recommend, where this is the case, that you advise the employment agency that your resume is not to be mailed to any association members without your specific approval and, under no circumstances, is it to be made available to the general association membership.

In addition to the obvious risk of being found out by your current employer, there is also the danger that a given employer will receive several copies of your resume from different sources. This mass broadcasting suggests to potential employers that your job campaign lacks focus and control. It also suggests that you are not using proper discretion and care in conducting your campaign if, as your resume suggests, you are currently employed. This may also suggest that perhaps you no longer have need to be concerned about being found out by your current employer (e.g., have already been terminated). Thus, as you can see, it is important to control distribution of your resume.

As a final caution, since employment agency fees are not always paid by the employer, it is important, when accepting the opportunity for an interview with one of the agency's client companies, to determine whether this company is willing to pay the agency fee if you are subsequently hired by that firm. These fees are substantial and should not be taken lightly. The norm is one percent for every $1,000 of the first year's annual compensation (maximum fee of 30 percent). Thus, a position paying $40,000 could have an agency fee of $12,000; a $50,000 job a fee of $15,000; an $80,000 job a fee of $24,000, etc. Although most companies will pay the agency fee for hiring professional or managerial talent, this is not always the case. Considering the size of these fees, this is not an item to be left to chance.

If you have difficulty in identifying a half dozen or so employment managers from whom you can secure recommendations on the more reputable employment agencies, a suitable alternative might be to secure references from the agency itself. Ask the agency representative, with whom you would be working, for the names of four or five employment managers with whom they have worked on a regular basis. Tell him or her that you would like to talk with these references before establishing a working relationship. By all means, check these references carefully before proceeding to work with the firm. Here are some questions you could use to check these references:

1. How long have you dealt with the ABC Agency?

2. What has been the nature of this association?

3. How satisfied have you been with their thoroughness and professionalism?

4. What criticisms, if any, might you have concerning their performance?

5. Have you had much occasion to work with Consultant X?

6. What has been the nature of that working relationship?

7. What observations can you make about Consultant X's thoroughness and professionalism?

8. From your observations, what are his/her strengths?

9. What are his or her shortcomings, if any?

10. If you were considering a job change, would you use his or her services? Why? Why not?

Answers to these questions should put you in a position to know whether this is the type of firm with which you should be working. It is important to the success of your campaign that you be represented by persons who will be thorough, professional, and have your career interests at heart. You certainly want to avoid money-hungry hucksters who will try to sell your soul to the first bidder for a quick buck, so don't short-cut this reference checking procedure. Know that the persons who will be representing you can be trusted and will accurately represent both your qualifications and interests to prospective employers.

If you are uncertain about how to identify employment agencies with specialization in your industry or profession, there are a few things that you can do to flush this out. Some of the better sources for securing this information are the various trade or professional journals relating to your areas of interest. You will find that many of the better agencies, having specialization in these areas, will advertise in these highly-targeted publications. The officers of trade and professional associations will usually know who the key players are. They can also suggest the journals, relating to their fields, that are likely to contain recruitment ads of these specialty agencies. So, with a few well-placed phone calls, you will be able to quickly identify the firms with whom you should definitely be in contact.

It is important, however, that you not overestimate the importance of employment agencies as an employment source. Various studies conclude that only between nine and twelve percent of all jobs filled in the United States are filled by employment agencies. If you are a serious job hunter, it is important that you not rely solely on the use of employment agencies, but rather make use of a wide array of employment sources when conducting your job search campaign.

EXECUTIVE SEARCH FIRMS

Although you should certainly not overlook the use of executive search firms when conducting your job search, you should not overestimate potential results. Search firms are thought to fill only about 2 to 5 percent of all job openings. Typically they focus on filling higher middle management and executive level positions only. Thus, if you seek a lower level management or professional level position, you could waste your time by contacting these firms. In such cases, although these firms are usually highly professional, they are less likely to be able to help you than the employment agencies.

When your resume hits the door, the odds are great that the search firm will not currently be working on an assignment that is related to your qualifications and interests. Since, by the nature of their business, they represent the employer rather than the job seeker, you can be reasonably assured that, unless they just coincidentally have an assignment that matches your background, you will not be hearing from them. The most you can expect is that you will receive a brief letter or postcard acknowledging receipt of your resume and notifying you that they are not currently working on an assignment conducive to your interests.

Although the odds are against you, there may still be good reasons for sending your resume to executive search firms. This is particularly true if you are employed in a management capacity and have 1992 earnings of $70,000 or higher. Currently, many of the better executive search firms have a salary cutoff of $70,000 and will not conduct search assignments for client companies where the compensation level of the position is below the $70,000 level. Thus, if you are earning considerably below this level, don't waste your time. By contrast, if you are employed in a management or executive position and are earning over $70,000

(1992 basis), it is recommended that you make a sizeable (over 500 pieces) broadcast mailing of your resume to these firms. My experience shows that such a mailing, during reasonable economic times, will normally yield a 3 to 5 percent return. Even if there is no suitable opening available at the time of your inquiry, should you have good credentials, you can be assured that your resume will be filed for reference in the event a future search assignment is undertaken by the firm that is a suitable match for your qualifications and interests.

Unlike the employment agency, you do not have to be concerned that the search firm will mail your resume all over the place. To the contrary, they will not normally present a candidate's credentials to a client company without first conducting an indepth, face-to-face interview, followed by a thorough check of references. You are assured of your confidentiality and there is therefore little risk in forwarding your credentials to these firms. Additionally, since the consulting fees of the executive search firm are always paid by the client company whom they serve, there is absolutely no cost to you, should this contact result in your employment by the client organization.

There is one word of caution when it comes to dealing with executive search firms: *Beware of impostors!* Unfortunately, it has become popular for employment agencies to refer to themselves as executive search firms, when in fact they are not. This practice has served to seriously blur the distinction between the two in the mind of the public. The acid test has to do with the method by which these firms are compensated for their services.

The true executive search consulting firm works only on a fully retained basis. As consultants, they are compensated for their consulting time, regardless of the outcome of the search assignments. Normally their fees range between 30 and 35 percent of the estimated first year's annual compensation of a successful candidate. These fees are usually paid by the client company in three equal installments over the first three months of the search assignment. If cancellation of the assignment occurs within these first three months, the total fee is prorated accordingly and the search firm is compensated for actual time spend on the search.

Employment agencies fall into two categories based upon how they are compensated—contingency firms and retained contingency. As the term suggests, agencies who work on a contingency basis are only entitled to a fee (from either the candidate or the company) when they have successfully placed a candidate in the job. Such firms have not been retained by the client organization, and the client organization, therefore, has no legal obligation whatsoever to pay the agent's fee. In such case, the job seeker can be very much at risk, and may end up with a legal obligation to pay the agency fee if successfully placed with an employer.

The retained contingency firms, although still technically an employment agency, usually have a much stronger working relationship with the client company. These firms usually require the client firm, who has retained their services, to pay a portion (usually one-third) of their fee at the onset of the assignment, with the balance (usually two-thirds) to be paid contingent upon successful placement of a candidate in the position. Here again, as with the contingency agency, they are not truly consultants and are thus principally compensated on the basis of results rather than their consulting time.

Hopefully this discussion has clarified the difference between the employment agency and the executive search firm. It should also be clear that the executive search firms generally stand at the top of their profession, are very knowledgeable and professional, and are compensated as professional consultants for their consulting time.

What does all of this have to do with your job search? Simply this: If you want to avoid the risk of having your resume plastered like wallpaper all over the place, you will want to avoid indiscriminately mailing it out to employment agencies. You must therefore know how to tell the difference between the agency and the search firm (to whom you will clearly want to mail your resume). Additionally, it is important to make this distinction so that you are not suddenly surprised with the possible presentation of a rather sizeable bill for the agent's services.

The trick is to secure a listing of the fully retained executive search firms to be included in your mail campaign. Fortunately, many of these firms belong to one of two organizations. The first is the AESC (Association of Executive Search Consultants), headquartered in Greenwich, Connecticut. The second, a newer organization, is the NACPR (National Association of Corporate and Professional Recruiters), headquartered in Stamford, Connecticut. The NACPR has offices throughout the United States, and can be located by calling information in some of the larger cities (New York, Philadelphia, Boston, etc.). You should contact both of these associations to see how you might secure a copy of their membership directory.

Another excellent source is *The Directory of Executive Recruiters* published by Kennedy Publications in Fitzwilliam, New Hampshire. This directory lists over 2,000 search firms and employment agencies. All, however, according to it's Editor, Jim Kennedy, charge their client companies for their fees. Also, Kennedy has separated the listing into 2 distinct categories— retainer firms and contingency firms—for your convenience. The phone number for Kennedy Publications is (603) 585-2200.

When mailing your resume to executive search firms, be sure to mail copies to all offices of each firm, not just the firm's corporate offices. Don't assume because they are the firm's corporate offices that your resume will automatically be available to other regional offices. This may not be the case and you could easily eliminate consideration of your employment candidacy for a highly desirable position being handled by one of the firm's branch offices.

Likewise, if you are unwilling to relocate or otherwise have geographical restrictions, don't simply mail your resume to the regional office closest to your desired geographical area. In most cases, consultants of executive search firms are not limited to working in a certain geographical region. Instead, they tend to be functional or industry specialists, and work with clients on a national, if not international, basis. Thus, a consultant working out of the San Francisco office is likely to have clients located in Philadelphia, New York, or Atlanta, and although unlikely, may not have a single client in the San Francisco area.

Although many career counselors and outplacement firms may advise you differently, I do not recommend making *cold calls* to the offices of executive search consulting firms. You would do better with a dart board at a hundred yards. Most consultants simply refuse to take unsolicited calls from job seekers. The experienced ones have long ago come to realize that taking such calls is a poor use of their time. Additionally, your time can be more constructively utilized by focusing on other sources that are likely to prove productive in achieving your job search objectives. Send your resume. Don't call. You will hear soon enough if the consultant has a search assignment for which you are a possible candidate. Calling to discuss your background, when it is extremely unlikely that the consultant is currently working on an appropriate search assignment, is hardly an effective use of valuable time. Don't call. Invest your time and energy elsewhere.

ALUMNI ASSOCIATIONS

Many colleges and universities offer employment or placement services to their alumni. In the case of larger schools, there is often an alumni placement office set up for this very purpose. Some of these are quite active and maintain close ties with major employers who frequently recruit on their campus for recent college graduates.

In most cases the alumni placement office serves as clearing house for resumes submitted by its alumni. Employers list job openings with the alumni placement office, whose staff then compares the requirements of these positions with resumes of alumni on file, forwarding the resumes of qualified persons to the listing employer. Placement can sometimes result.

This source, although not normally very productive, seems to work best where the school has strong recruiting relationships with the employer, and the firm has had a long history of recruiting graduates from a particular curriculum. For instance, if the school has long had an excellent reputation for its curriculum in Packaging Engineering, and there are a number of companies who recruit there for that purpose, there is a high likelihood that when the same companies are in need of an experienced packaging engineer, they will think of this school as a potential source and contact the alumni placement office.

With the exception of those schools who enjoy an excellent reputation for a given educational discipline, alumni placement offices are not usually very productive job sources, and should not be thought of as a major employment source when planning your job search campaign. They can occasionally be helpful, so should not be ignored altogether.

A quick phone call to your alma mater is all that it takes to determine if it provides job placement assistance to its alumni. Inquire about the necessary procedures on how to get your resume into their system and then send them a copy.

JOB FAIRS AND RECRUITING CONFERENCES

The job fair or recruiting conference has long been a tool used by companies to recruit hard-to-find talent. Most often, it has been used by the aerospace, defense electronics, and computer industries to recruit hard-to-find technical talent (engineers, scientists, computer programmers, etc.). They have also been used, however, as a method for the recruitment of persons with generic skills that can be applied across companies and industries (accounting, sales, etc.). For the most part, such conferences are used by participating companies as a way to fill junior level organization openings (i.e., those requiring one to five years of experience).

Job fairs and recruiting conferences have been organized by both employers (especially when they have a number of similar openings) and individual entrepreneurs, who are motivated by profit. In most cases there is no fee charged to the candidate participants. Instead, employers who are participating are required to pay a base registration for participation in the conference, plus a fee for each successful hiring that results from conference interviews. In some cases, however, the candidate applicant may also be charged a registration fee, as well. It's best to determine what your financial obligations will be in advance of your participation. In this way, there are no surprises later on.

One of the key attractions of a job fair or recruiting conference is that it potentially provides you with the opportunity to interview with more than one employer in the span of a one- or two-day period. It is advisable to find out what the interview ground rules are in advance of your attendance, so that you are not disappointed.

In some conferences, employers are permitted closed schedules. This means they have the opportunity to prescreen the resumes of attendees in advance (or at the beginning) of the conference, designating to the conference managers which of the candidates they wish to interview. In such cases they are under no obligation to interview any other conference participants. Thus, if it is a closed schedule conference, you may or may not have the opportunity to interview with those employers in whom you have the most interest.

An open schedule conference means that you have the opportunity to sign up with any of the conference attendees, and, provided there is space on their interview schedule, they are obligated to grant you an employment interview. An open schedule may be more to your advantage; however, this would depend upon the employers who are scheduled to be in attendance.

Prior to investing in registration fees and the expenses of travel and lodging, it would pay to do some advance research.

Call the group responsible for organization and management of the conference and ask the following questions:

1. What are the fees for registration?

2. What fees, if any, will be payable by you, should you be hired by one of the employers attending the conference?

3. How many employers will be attending the conference?

4. Which, if any, are firms from your job search target group?

5. What are the positions for which these firms will be recruiting?

6. Are the interview sign-up schedules closed or open?

7. If closed schedules, when and how do you determine which employers have expressed an interest in you?

8. How many candidates will be in attendance at the conference?

Generally speaking, the better conferences are those where all costs are borne by the employers who are in attendance. A willingness to pay all conference and resultant placement fees by the employer is usually a good sign that the employers feel that such conferences are a valuable source of employment candidates. Such employer willingness to pay these fees is also usually a sign that the firms who will be in attendance are worthwhile, rather than fly-by-night organizations.

Be somewhat wary of those conferences where the fees are to be borne by the candidate attendees. Such arrangements usually suggest that the conference sponsors are more interested in collecting fees from attendees than doing something meaningful that will result in solid employment opportunities. If in doubt, ask for the names, and contact information from four or five attendees who attended the last conference sponsored by this group. Make sure you are investing your time and money wisely.

If you are interested in finding out more about career conferences or job fairs that focus on your industry or professional specialty, a good source can be the national office of your trade or professional association. They are usually aware of who the sponsoring organizations are and how to contact them. Also, sponsoring organizations often advertise upcoming job fairs and career conferences in the trade journals and newsletters related to the industry or professional specialty they are targeting. These conferences are also frequently advertised in major metropolitan newspapers in the want ad section.

COMPUTER JOB BANKS

The origin of computer job banks dates back at least 20 to 25 years. The underlying concept behind these banks is the ability to use the computer to match applicant qualification to a preloaded list of jobs specifications, thus being able to identify qualified candidates for these positions.

Computer job banks, for the most part, have been the brainchild of entrepreneurial individuals who saw this as a concept for making lots of money. The idea is to market this system both ways—to the job seeker as well as the employer. Typically the job seeker is charged a registration fee (ranging from $25 to several hundred dollars) for the privilege of inputting basic data extracted from a resume into the computer data base. On the other side of the ledger, companies are then charged a fee to access this data base to search out persons having certain qualifications. For this, they may pay a one-time access fee or a general access fee that entitles them to access the database for a defined period (usually a year).

Every time I think of these candidate search data bases, I am reminded of the time a vendor of such a system, who shall remain nameless, came to my office at Scott Paper Company to demonstrate his wares. (At the time, I worked in the Corporate Employment Department as Manager of Technical Employment.) At the time of this vendor's visit, we were in the process of recruiting a large number of engineers to staff a major $1.3 billion capital expansion project.

The vendor represented a very large, multibillion dollar company, who decided that this would be an effective way to market a voluminous data base of engineering talent that they had accumulated as a result of their own recruiting efforts. The vendor had with him a desktop computer and modum which could be used to access the database in the firm's main computer, back at corporate headquarters. Although time has blurred my memory a bit (this was 1975), I believe that the data base contained somewhere in excess of 25,000 engineers.

After some initial difficulty in hooking up the computer and accessing the main data base, my guest then proceeded to conduct a live test of how this database was supposed to work. Taking one of the positions for which I was recruiting (which, by the way, required a fairly generic profile), I provided the vendor with about 14 or 15 selection factors, each of which was diligently inputted into the system. The vendor then gave the computer the necessary command to commence search of the data base for our candidate. After a few seconds of search, a message appeared on the screen to the effect that no such candidate existed within the database. We then repeated the search four or five times, each time using fewer and fewer of the original 14 or 15 selection criteria.

Finally, after several false starts, we were able to generate a printout of available candidates, each with a brief biographical summary of qualifications. By now, however, the list of selection criteria used on the final search was so watered down, compared to the original selection criteria, that the list of candidates generated was almost meaningless. Additionally, the data provided on each supposedly qualified candidate was so general that it was impossible to tell for such whether the candidates were truly viable for the position we were trying to fill. We then repeated the experiment using several other positions and specifications with similar results. In each case, there were few, if any, candidates identified. Where identified, there was insufficient information available about the candidate upon which to base a decision. The next step would have been to request a hard copy of each candidate's resume, which would have been sent to us by mail. This was hardly a timesaving, efficient system. Needless to say, we elected not to subscribe to this network.

This story serves to illustrate a point. Although computers, I'm sure, have advanced to the point of having the capability to handle such a system, to the best of my knowledge no one has developed a sufficiently good system to make this application a truly viable concept. Typically, the problems with such databases are:

1. Insufficient number of candidate entries to make the system attractive to employer users.

2. Insufficient number of job entries to make the system attractive to candidate users.

3. The time and cost necessary to keep candidate and job listings current is usually prohibitive, thus resulting in a database that is chock-full of obsolete data.

4. The number of candidate or job selection criteria variables is enormous, making it difficult to input sufficient information to allow for meaningful identification and selection. (Results are poor matching or insufficient data upon which to make a good decision.)

Recent development of improved software coupled with the ever improving technology of page scanners suggests that it will not be long before viable resume databases are available to both the job seeker and employer. So, keep alert to this possibility.

In the meantime, if tempted to make use of a computerized job bank, before paying your access fee I would suggest that you get answers to the following basic questions:

1. How many total employers are represented in the job bank?

2. How many of these employers are from your target industries?

3. How current is the database?

4. What is the system for maintaining the database?

5. What is the basis for selecting jobs for entry (i.e., what is the source of jobs; what are the criteria for entry)?

6. How frequently are new listings inputted?

7. What is the basis for purging listings from the database?

8. How often is data purged?

9. What are the variables which can be used for screening the database? What are the limitations?

10. What are the access fees?

11. What is the frequency and limitations on access?

12. Will the vendor provide a demonstration (using unrelated position, of course)?

A similar set of questions needs to be asked if the database is one that lists candidates, as opposed to jobs. The presumption here is that the database will be used by employers to identify candidates for current openings within their organization. These questions are:

1. How many total employers are currently subscribers to the data base?

2. How many of these are from target industries?

3. How many job seekers are contained in the data base?

4. What is the breakout of functional disciplines represented by these candidates?

5. Does the data base focus on industry, or functional specialties, or is it a general data base?

6. What has been the frequency of employer inquiries of the data base? In the last year? In the last month?

7. How current is the data base?

8. How often is it purged?

9. What determines when a candidate's file is purged?

10. What are the fees for inputting your data?

11. Exactly what information will be inputted from your resume? What is excluded?

12. How long will our information remain on file in the data base?

13. What safeguards exist that would prevent disclosure of your information to your current employer, should your employer or any of its affiliates have access to the database?

If currently employed, one major danger of using this kind of candidate database as part of your job hunting campaign is the danger that your employer may discover that you are on the job market. It is particularly important, therefore, that there be safeguards in effect that would prevent release of your computer file to either your current employer or to one of its affiliate companies. Additionally, if access to the data base is not controlled and, for example, employment agencies are allowed access, your risks are substantially increased. It is, therefore, your responsibility to determine the types of controls that are exercised by the data base manager to prevent this unnecessary risk and potentially embarrassing exposure.

To date, computer job banks have not proven a highly effective job hunting source. There are simply too many limitations and risks associated with them to make them very useful. Although you might want to use them to supplement other more viable sources, don't count on them to play a major role in your job hunting campaign.

CAREER CONSULTANTS

The field of career and job search consulting is exploding. The recent downsizing of the middle management segment of American industry, coupled with sweetened early retirement and separation programs, has caused a flood of middle management and seasoned professionals on the job market. Most of these are people needing job hunting assistance of some type, ranging all the way from resume preparation assistance to the planning of full-fledged job search marketing programs with all the bells and whistles. Many of these managers and professionals have not been on the job markets for 15 to 20 years and, for the most part, are at a total loss on how to organize and plan an effective job hunting campaign.

Along with this demand for employment assistance, has come the birth and explosion of an entirely new industry—the outplacement consulting practice. Only a decade ago, the idea of companies paying sizeable fees to consultants for providing job hunting training and assistance to terminated employees, was almost unheard of. At that time, assistance, if provided at all, was usually limited to some basic counseling on resume preparation, and rudimentary job hunting techniques provided by the employer's personnel or employment manager. For older, seasoned employees who have been out of the job market for several years, such basic counseling proved woefully inadequate with the consequence that many of these employees were months in making a successful employment transition (if ever).

In recent years with the current emphasis on employee headcount reduction as an important method of cost reduction and achievement of competitive advantage, the concept of company-paid outplacement job hunting assistance has come of age. Motivated by a combination of social responsibility and the threat of expensive litigation from terminated employees, many companies now employ professional outplacement consultants to run full-fledged job search training programs for their terminated employees. There are company-sponsored outplacement centers that house and nurture these employees during the sometimes lengthy and arduous job hunting process. For this, they can pay these consultants rather sizeable fees ranging from a couple of hundred dollars for simple resume preparation assistance, to several thousand dollars for a highly-individualized job search planning and support program. Fees charged for more elaborate programs can run as high as 10 to 15 percent of the terminated employee's annual salary, plus reimbursement of the consultant's out-of-pocket expenses. Thus the outplacement fee for a $100,000 executive could run as high as $10,000 to $15,000.

Although many of these professional outplacement consulting firms provide their services only to employers, some will undertake individual counseling, as well. This can be a fairly expensive proposition, so you will want to be sure of what you are getting for your money. For the most part, professional, reputable firms offer a fairly comprehensive service including:

1. Some minor psychological counseling to assist you in making the transition from being employed to being unemployed, and to put you into a positive frame of mind as you begin the job hunting process

2. Some career and job counseling aimed at helping you to define realistic, obtainable job hunting objectives

3. Assistance in preparing a professional, effective resume

4. Training in the use of numerous job hunting and job reference sources

5. Training in the use of various job hunting techniques (especially emphasizing the networking process)

6. Training in effective interviewing techniques (along with practice interviews followed by professional critique)

7. Use of a professional job search center including all support services (library, phones, typing, and secretarial support)

8. Continued counseling and support throughout the job search process, as needed

In addition to these professional outplacement firms, which generally provide their services to corporations, there have been a whole host of employment and career counseling firms that have sprung up to meet the needs of the individual job seeker. The more reputable ones provide training and services substantially similar to those provided by the outplacement consultant. Unfortunately, along with these ethical and reputable firms, numerous less reputable firms have emerged to fill the void. These purveyors of snake oil and quick-fix bromides have one thing in common: They are out to dazzle you with their fancy footwork and lighten your wallet, without providing you with any meaningful job hunting assistance.

I have been involved with the job hunting process, in one way or another, for over 25 years, and believe me when I say, "There are no shortcuts to the job search process." Successful job hunting requires three things: patience, persistence, and plenty of hard work. There are no quick, easy fixes that will allow you to short-cut the process and find meaningful employment in a short time frame. As testimony to this, consider the fact that most knowledgeable employment professionals estimate that, on average, it takes about one month of job search time for every $10,000 of annual earnings to find a meaningful job. Thus, an executive earning $100,000 can expect to look for ten months; a $60,000 executive, six months; a $40,000 professional, four months, etc. The logic behind this says, the higher the job level, the fewer are the jobs at this level, and the longer it takes to find such a position. Conversely, the lower the job level, the more plentiful are the jobs and the shorter is the job search.

Beware of those consultants who claim they can help you find a job quickly, or who claim they have some magical method for helping you to find that job that you've always dreamed of. Also, beware of the gimmicks—things like exclusive lists of key openings, elaborate computer matching services, special inside contacts who will help get interviews, special computer mailing lists of key contacts, etc. Generally, the more ludicrous the claim, the higher the probability that you'll be dealing with a crook who is a sure expert in one area only—parting you from your hard-earned money.

Don't fall for gimmickry. Plain and simply, successful job hunting requires nothing less than good old persistence and hard work. So, keep your money in your pocket and follow the advice in this book.

If you do feel compelled to use the services of a professional job search consultant, take the time to check the firm out. Make sure that the firm is completely above board and that your money is going to be well-spent. To be sure that you are dealing with a reputable firm, before spending any money, get answers to the following questions:

1. How long has the firm been in business?

2. How many persons have they counseled over the years?

3. What has been their success rate? How many of their clients have found meaningful work? What has been the average length of time needed to find work?

4. What are the total fees?

5. What do you get for your investment (i.e., the components of their program)?

6. What are the qualifications of your counselor(s)?

7. What direct employment experience has this counselor(s) had (e.g., search firm, employment manager, employment agency), if any?

8. What guarantees, if any, do they provide?

If you get relatively good answers to these questions and feel that you might wish to go ahead with their service, take one additional step—ask for references. Request the names and contact information on at least four or five persons who have recently gone through their program. If you are told that the names of their clients are confidential and they can, therefore, not honor your request, tell them to contact these clients and get permission to release this information to you. If they balk at this request, I have one final piece of advice: Hang on to your wallet and get out of there as fast as you can!

On the other hand, if the consultant provides you with the references that you have requested, make sure to check them thoroughly before proceeding. Here are some suggested questions that might be used in doing this:

1. If you don't mind sharing this information with me, what did you pay for the services of the ABC Company?

2. What, specifically, did you get for your money?

3. Overall, how would you rate their program?

4. In what areas did the program meet or exceed your expectations?

5. In what areas did the program fall short of your expectations?

6. In what ways could the program have been made more meaningful?

7. If you knew what you now know about this program, would you take it again? Why?

8. Was it a good value for the money, or is it overpriced?

As a final step, having completed this reference check, contact the local Better Business Bureau to find out whether there have been any recent complaints filed against the company in question. If so, how many and what have been the nature of these complaints? Additionally, you might contact some of the personnel and employment managers working for area companies to find out what they can tell you about the company.

If a thorough reference check turns up little or no negative information, chances are you are safe to proceed, and that you will be getting a quality service for your money. In general, however, you can probably do just as much for yourself by reading a couple of good books on the subject of job hunting. Most of what these firms offer to do in the form of consulting services can be done by you, and you can save a lot of money in the process.

BUSINESS CONSULTING FIRMS

Firms engaged in providing consulting services to companies (i.e., strategic planning, marketing, accounting, financial, and human resource consulting) are many times aware of potential job openings long before these openings hit the street. Such firms can therefore prove to be a noteworthy source for identifying new job opportunities.

Unfortunately, unless you have a close personal contact with the consulting firm, these advance leads may be extremely difficult to get. Since these firms are privy to a great deal of confidential information regarding such things as new products, new market strategy, acquisitions, joint ventures, capital expansions, etc., they are often aware of the possibility of opportunities. In many cases, because of this confidentiality, however, they are not at liberty to share this information with you. There is nothing to stop them from recommending you or passing your resume along to the right party, however.

As part of your employment strategy, therefore, it would probably be a good idea to cultivate some friendships with principals or consultants employed by these types of consulting firms.

BANKS AND ATTORNEYS

As with consulting firms, banks and attorneys are often aware of organizational changes that could result in staffing needs within client organizations. With this in mind, it is probably a good idea, when possible, to cultivate some relationships in these type firms, as well. These relationships could lead to a personal recommendation or job lead referral.

STATE EMPLOYMENT SERVICE

The State Employment Service, known within some states as the Bureau of Employment Security, has, as its main purpose, the objective of helping unemployed workers to find employment. The laws in many states requires employers to list all job openings with the State Employment Service so these positions can be listed on a master list for use by the state's employment counselors. Sometimes, these lists are computerized, and it is possible to use the computer to search the list for job openings that may be appropriate to your background and interests.

Although in many states the law provides for mandatory listing of job openings, my impression is that this is not often well-policed and, as a result, many openings never appear on the list. Nonetheless, as part of your job search campaign, it is probably a good idea to visit the State Employment Service to find out what resources are available to help you in your job search. Although, historically, the states have been far more successful in finding jobs for blue collar workers, there is always the possibility that some real assistance could be forthcoming. In any event, access to the computerized job bank may be just the thing that makes this a worthwhile trip.

This, like the alumni placement office, is another one of those free services that should not be overlooked as you plan and execute your job search strategy. As the saying goes, *Check your telephone directory for the office nearest you.*

10

The Direct Mail Campaign

Use of the direct mail campaign is a fairly common job hunting technique that has been around for quite a number of years. If carefully designed and executed, it can be a productive source of interviews and employment opportunities. (Generally, surveys have shown that the overall response rate to direct mail campaigns of this sort is somewhere in the 1 percent to 3 percent range.) The key words here are *designed* and *executed.* If little time and effort are put into the design and execution of this job search method, it can be a complete waste of time.

Who should use a direct mail campaign? When should it be used? How is an effective campaign planned and executed? What are the steps needed to ensure success? This chapter will provide answers to these questions as well as a step-by-step process for designing and executing an effective campaign. If carefully followed, the advice provided here should enable you to design your own direct mail campaign and to effectively target it to help you in achieving your job search objective.

No job hunting method or technique can guarantee good results. The direct mail campaign is no exception to this rule and, at most, will provide only a partial answer to your job hunting needs. It makes sense, therefore, to view this as only one component of your total job hunting program. It should, by no means, represent your sole method for finding employment.

WHEN TO USE THE DIRECT MAIL CAMPAIGN

The direct mail campaign is generally used by those who are currently employed, and cannot commit a significant amount of time to the job search process. One of the key advantages of this technique is that it is a method that can be planned and executed during evenings and weekends, which does not interfere with one's work schedule. It is commonly used as a substitute for the networking process (described in the next chapter) by those who simply cannot expend the necessary time to carry out a full-blown networking process.

It is the opinion of this author, and one that is shared by most employment and outplacement professionals, that networking is, by far, a much more effective job search technique than is the mail campaign. In fact, surveys show that networking accounts for about 70 percent of all jobs found. Unfortunately, however, networking is very time consuming, and does not lend itself well to those who are currently employed. From a practical standpoint, employed persons don't normally have the necessary freedom to make the numerous telephone calls and personal contacts that are essential to making the networking process a success. The direct mail campaign must therefore play a much larger role in the employed individual's job hunting campaign.

This does not mean that employed persons should ignore the networking process. To the contrary, they should clearly use it as a job hunting method. Time constraints will dictate, however, that networking will play a substantially reduced role in the total search process of those who are employed. Conversely, by virtue of these same constraints, the mail campaign will assume a much larger role.

The direct mail campaign should certainly not be ignored as a job hunting method by those who are currently unemployed. It is an effective method that can be used to supplement the networking process. Since networking has historically proven itself to be a far more productive method than the direct mail campaign, however, those who are unemployed should place less emphasis on the mail campaign and commit the bulk of their time to the networking technique. In such cases, the direct mail campaign should be used only as a means of contacting those target firms where, after considerable effort, it was not possible to use personal contacts to network. It should also be used as a supplemental technique to contact secondary target companies, where, due to the size of the primary target group, personal contact with these secondary firms is not a practical consideration.

Whether employed or unemployed, the direct mail campaign should be included in all job hunting campaigns. In both cases, the method for planning and executing an effective mail campaign is identical.

KEY STEPS

The key steps of an effective mail campaign are fairly straight forward. They are:

1. Design of cover letter

2. Research of target industry (or geography)

3. Identification of target executive

4. Actual mailing

We will use this chapter to systematically explore each of these components and to make suggestions which should help to increase the effectiveness of this employment search technique. By following each of these steps, in the sequence provided, you should be able to plan and execute an effective direct mail campaign.

Designing the Cover Letter

Design of an effective cover letter for a broadcast campaign need not be a particularly difficult task. Essentially, the letter is comprised of the following elements:

1. Return address

2. Date

3. Employer's name and address

4. Salutation

5. Introductory paragraph

6. Statement of purpose

7. Brief summary of qualifications

8. Request for response

9. Closing and signature

Some sample broadcast cover letters are provided at the end of this chapter. Study them carefully and use them as models for designing your own cover letter for use with your direct mail campaign.

Research Methodology

Once you have designed an effective broadcast cover letter for use in your direct mail campaign, your next step is to research your primary target industry to develop a list of target companies for your mailing list. There are several good sources that can be used for this purpose. These are:

1. *Thomas' Register*

   Thomas Publishing Company, 461 Eighth Avenue, New York, New York 10001.

   Lists 100,000 manufacturers by product and location.

2. *Moody's Industrial Manual, Volume One*

   Moody's Investment Service, 99 Church Street, New York, New York 10007.

   Provides a classification of thousands of companies by industries and products.

3. *Directories in Print*

   Gale Research Company, Book Tower, Detroit, Michigan 48226.

   Lists over 5,000 directories classified into 15 major classifications and more than 2,100 subject headings. Directory categories include industry, business, education, government, science, and public affairs.

4. *National Trade and Professional Associations of the United States*

   Columbia Books Inc., Publishers, 1350 New York Avenue, N.W., Suite 207, Washington, D.C. 20005

   Lists about 6,500 national trade associations; labor unions; professional, scientific, or technical societies; and other national organizations.

5. *Encyclopedia of Associations*

   Gale Research Company, Book Tower, Detroit, Michigan 48226.

   Lists over 1,200 trade and professional associations serving the U.S.

6. *State Industrial Directories*

Available at major libraries, state chambers of commerce, and state employment security offices. Provide a comprehensive listing of nearly every company that does business within the state. Each company is assigned a Standard Industrial Classification (S.I.C.) number; defines the product(s) manufactured.

7. *Chamber of Commerce Directories*

Many city and area chambers of commerce publish directories similar to the state industrial directories, but geographically restricted to areas they serve. These can normally be acquired at nominal cost.

During the research phase of your project, target companies can usually be identified using these reference sources. Most of the directories can be used to directly identify specific target companies. Others are used as resources to identify industrial and trade associations, from which membership directories can be acquired for a minimal fee. Many times target companies belong to such trade associations, and membership directories may be borrowed by simply contacting someone you know who is employed with one of these target companies.

With a day or two of good research using these sources, you can develop a comprehensive listing of target companies to be used as the basis for your mail campaign.

Identifying Target Executives

When preparing your mailing list, it is most important to identify not only the names of target companies but also the names and titles of specific executives and managers to whom your mailing will be sent. This type of pinpoint mailing is more likely to generate a positive response than one that is simply sent to a functional department within the organization.

When researching the names of target executives, there is one important rule to keep in mind: Don't send your mailing to the Personnel or Employment Department. These departments, although sometimes well-organized and highly professional, are not always aware of potential new openings that may develop. It is better to send your cover letter and resume to a manager who heads the functional area for which you are applying. These persons are more keenly aware of the business problems and dynamics that can spawn the need for additional human resources, specific technical skills, etc. Sometimes the receipt of a well-prepared cover letter and resume is just the thing that triggers the decision to hire. I have seen this happen time and time again.

When doing your research, try to identify the person in the organization who, by job title and organizational level, is likely to be the person to whom you would report if you were hired by this organization. Thus, if you are a production manager, target the operations manager; if an operations manager, target the director of manufacturing; if a director of manufacturing, target the vice president of manufacturing; and so on. When job titles are confusing, and you are in doubt as to which position to pick, select the functional head of the area for which you are applying. If your mailing hits at too high an organizational level, chances are that it will be passed down to the right organization level.

When you are in a more senior management position (i.e., senior manager, director, vice president), this part of the research can be fairly easy. Many industrial directories furnish the names and titles of persons at the director levels and above. When you are in a middle management, junior management, or professional level position, however, things are a bit tougher. In such cases you will need to dig a little harder and a little deeper to get the information that you need.

For these more junior level positions, the professional and trade association directories are useful sources of information. Many of these associations publish membership directories that list not only companies, but individual members as well. In many cases, these individual members are listed two ways:

(1) Alphabetically, by last name, and (2) Alphabetically, under the name of the company with whom they are employed. Here is a process you can use to identify these people:

1. Use the *National Trade and Professional Associations of the United States* and the *Encyclopedia of Associations* as your key sources.

2. Identify the trade associations to which your target companies are likely to belong.
    a. Contact trade associations to determine if a membership directory is published.
    b. Determine if this directory lists the names and titles of individual members (in addition to company membership).
    c. Where individual memberships are listed, order copy of directory. (Note: If distribution of directory is limited to association members only, you will need to identify a member and borrow a copy. To facilitate this, ask for contact information on area officers.)
    d. Use these trade membership directories to identify the names and titles of target executives for the target firms that you have chosen for your mailing.

3. Using the same reference sources as for trade associations, identify the professional associations and societies to which your target executives are most likely to belong.
    a. Contact these professional associations to determine if a membership directory is published.
    b. Order copy of directory for research purposes.
    c. Research the names and titles of target executives using these directories.

4. Use the *Directories in Print* to supplement search steps 1, 2, and 3 above.

a. Obtain appropriate trade association and professional association membership directories.

b. Research the names and titles of target executives using these directories.

If you have been fairly thorough and diligent with executing the steps of this research process, you will have been successful in identifying the names and titles of most target executives for the target firms that you are planning to include in your direct mail campaign. In those cases where you were not successful in identifying the specific person who occupies the organizational level targeted during your research, it is suggested that you forward your cover letter and resume to the vice president who heads the functional area in which you have an interest. If you are in manufacturing, use the vice president or director of manufacturing as your target person for mailing purposes. Such persons are normally more easily identified using one of the major industrial directories (e.g., *Dun & Bradstreet Million Dollar Directory, Dun & Bradstreet Middle Market Directory, Poor's Register of Corporation Directors & Executives, Standard Directory of Advertisers*).

You have now concluded the research portion of your direct mail campaign and are ready to proceed with the mailing itself.

The Mailing

To increase the probability that your letter will actually be received and read by the person whom you have targeted, it is best to type each envelope on an individual basis. Avoid the use of address labels since this smacks of a mass mailing, and is likely to get snagged by your target's secretary, who is frequently trained in the process of screening out all junk mail from the boss' mail folder.

To get away from this mass mail look, it is advisable to use envelopes made of quality stock. It may cost a little more, but it creates a professional and personalized impression. As an additional step to improving the probability of readership, type the word *CONFIDENTIAL* on either the front or back of the envelope. In some cases, use of this word may cause your letter to pass unopened from the secretary directly to the targeted executive.

At this point, you've done just about everything that you can do to design and execute an effective mail campaign. The next step is to sit back and see what it produces. Don't get your hopes up too high, since most experts say that such direct mail campaigns will usually generate not more than a one to three percent response rate. So for every 100 letters that you mail, you will probably get a response from only one to three companies. Quite frankly, in a tight employment market, you'll be doing very well to get this type of return. Keep in mind that it only takes one good inquiry to generate a job opportunity that is particularly attractive. So, hang in there! Your hard work might just pay off.

The next chapter deals with the subject of networking—a tried and proven technique for generating interview opportunities and job offers.

Broadcast Cover Letter

825 Stoney Hill Road
Portland, OR 17635
January 18, 1988

Ms. Mary Ann McQuail
President
Wharton Manufacturing Company
1771 Well Station Road
Dallas, Texas 98725

Dear Ms. McQuail:

As President and Chief Executive Officer of a leading firm in the field of hardware manufacturing, I am sure that you are aware of the importance and value of a top flight Chief Financial Officer on your staff. If you are in need of such an individual, you may wish to give serious consideration to my credentials.

With over 15 years of progressively senior accounting and financial management positions in the hardware manufacturing industry, I have logged some notable achievements in such important areas as cash flow improvement, profit enhancement, and improved management reporting, through application of modern computer software packages. In my current assignment as Chief Financial Officer for a $40 million manufacturer of industrial fasteners, for example, I initiated important programs that have earned nearly $2 million savings through modern cost tracking and targeting methods.

Although I have found my current position quite satisfying from the professional standpoint, Dutrar Company is family owned. For this reason, it would appear that future advancement opportunities may not be available. I have thus decided to search for a new professional position that offers better future growth possibilities.

My compensation requirements are in the $90,000 range plus comprehensive benefits package.

I would welcome the opportunity to explore appropriate opportunities with your firm, and would hope to hear from you in the near future.

Thank you for your consideration.

Sincerely,

Richard B. Smith

Broadcast Cover Letter

816 Clayton Avenue
Allentown, Pa 17365
December 17, 1978

Mr. Martin Clansberry
Director of Manufacturing
Carlston Tube Manufacturing, Inc.
127 First Street
Reading, CA 28736

Dear Mr. Clansberry:

A decision was recently made to close the Allentown plant of Falstrom Tube Company, where I have been employed as Operations Manager for the last five years. I am thus seeking a responsible position in manufacturing management with a company engaged in the manufacture of similar products, where my skills and extensive experience can be fully utilized.

My background includes over 20 years of experience in copper tubing manufacturing. This includes nearly 15 years in a management capacity. I have had an excellent record of consistently high level performance and meaningful contribution. In the last five years, for example, I have increased production output by nearly 18% while simultaneously reducing costs by 23%. I was cited for outstanding performance in 1976, and awarded the President's Award along with a sizeable bonus.

I hold an M.S. in Metallurgical Engineering and am up-to-date on modern manufacturing methodology. I am thoroughly trained and experienced in such concepts as total quality, statistical process control, and just in time management. I have also had experience working with new organization effectiveness and socio-technical management concepts.

I have no geographical preferences or restrictions. Salary requirements are in the mid $70,000 range and are negotiable, as appropriate, with the specific opportunity.

I look forward to hearing from you.

Sincerely,

Ralph F. Braun

Broadcast Cover Letter

142 East 42nd Street
Apartment 125
New York, New York 19873
October 24, 1987

Mr. Stephen Johnson
Vice President R & D
Dexter Pharmaceutical Company
875 Braxton Hollow Road
Springfield, MA 17635

Dear Mr. Johnson:

Because of your outstanding reputation as a leader in the field of biogenetic research, I am interested in exploring the possibility of employment as a senior scientist in your Research & Development function.

In addition to my technical qualifications as set forth in the enclosed resume, I feel that it is important for you to know that I have a reputation for creative solutions to the unusually difficult technical problems. I also possess the ability to translate market need into practical laboratory solutions. As a result, I enjoy an excellent reputation with marketing management for developing products uniquely suited to defined market requirements. This has greatly facilitated market planning and enabled the company to consistently achieve market objectives.

While I have enjoyed my employment with Diamond Chemical Company, the decision was recently made to sell the biotechnology division, the division with which I am employed. This impending sale, coupled with resultant future uncertainty, has prompted me to seek employment elsewhere.

My current compensation is in the low $70,000 range. I will require a comparable offer along with appropriate assistance with relocation costs.

Thank you for your consideration. I look forward to hearing from you shortly.

Sincerely,

Keith Larson

11

The Networking Process

Employment networking is by far the most important job hunting technique used today. In recent years, this technique has gotten considerable play and, today, stands as the undisputed centerpiece of most, if not all, professional outplacement employment training programs. It is the one employment strategy that seems to have the unanimous support of both seasoned employment and outplacement professionals alike. The reason for this is simple: It works!

Although admittedly a very effective job search method, the single largest drawback of the networking process is that it demands a considerable investment of personal time and discipline to execute it properly. It is for this reason that employed persons, who don't have the luxury of the time and freedom of those who are unemployed, find it difficult to adopt as their primary job search strategy. This is not to say that networking has no place in the employed person's job hunting campaign. It does! It simply means that, due to the practical constraints of time, it will need to take a back seat to other job hunting techniques that are a little less demanding.

By contrast, however, unemployed persons should make the networking process the core of their job search program. If well-planned and executed, this process can be extremely effective in surfacing job opportunities and interviews. With the proper investment of time and discipline, it has consistently proven to be a most valuable strategy.

What is employment networking? Who should use it? How does it work? What are the elements of the process? These, and other similar questions, will be answered in this chapter. In addition, this chapter will present you with a systematic, step-by-step method for implementing the employment networking process. If carefully followed, this process should prove very productive in your job hunting campaign.

WHAT IS EMPLOYMENT NETWORKING?

A network, by definition, is a group of things that are integrated and connected together to form a whole. In a figurative sense, it means anything that traps or ensnares, such as a web or a net. In a social sense, the term network has come to mean a process by which one reaches out to integrate and connect a group of friends for the purpose of securing their united support. The thing that is captured or ensnared is their assistance and support.

The social definition seems to fit the meaning of employment networking rather well. Employment networking is a process by which one reaches out to a group of friends and acquaintances for their ongoing support during the job hunting process. They are asked to provide their direct support by providing job leads and referrals, in addition to arranging for introduction to others who can also provide such leads and introductions. As more and more people are pulled in, and become active in supporting your job hunting campaign, the greater is the probability that the result will be job leads that will lead to employment interviews, and finally offers of employment.

Actually, the networking process is a bit like cell division. In cell division, each parent cell divides into two cells. These cells then also divide into two more (total of four cells). Each of the resultant four cells then divide into two (total eight cells), and so on, as this process continues to explode at a rapid rate. It is also like the familiar chain letter, where each person copies the letter and gives it to five friends, who copy it and give it to five more friends, who copy it and give it to five more friends, and so on. The outcome is a geometric progression where the number of contacts increase at an ever increasing rate.

The theory behind employment networking is somewhat similar and becomes a sort of geometric progression. By starting with a selected group of friends or acquaintances (say 50 or so), you ask them to help you identify a suitable job. Importantly, you also ask these same friends and acquaintances to provide you with the names of three to five of their friends whom you might contact to ask for their assistance. This second level group are then asked for their assistance, as well as the names of three to five of their acquaintances whom you might contact. Thus a geometric progression, much like cell division, is started and begins to grow at an increasing rate. Unlike cell division, however, the speed at which this progression grows is limited by your ability to contact all of the people who are identified by this process.

The beauty of this networking process is that you can start with a small group of friends and acquaintances and, with their cooperation, explode these contacts into several hundred in fairly short order. The initial group is known as the Level I or Primary Group. The group to whom this Primary Group refers you is the Level II or Secondary Group. The next group is called Level III, and so on. History has shown that few jobs are ever found through the Level I contacts. Instead, most jobs are found at the second, third and fourth levels. Thus, these contacts and subsequent referrals become very important to the success of the employment networking process.

As these contacts continue to expand and grow, so does the size of the social support net that you are building. The larger this net becomes, the more people are out there helping you on an ongoing basis. Sooner or later as the network continues to grow, you will begin to find job opportunities that are of interest to you.

Yes, this process really works! I've seen it work time and time again. I have personally had the opportunity to observe numerous persons use this process with a very high rate of success. In fact, of those who I have observed using this process, I have yet to see one failure.

Besides the obvious expanding number of persons who comprise the support group created by the networking process, what are the other factors that contribute to the success of this technique? There is one factor that is thought to significantly account for the success of the networking process. This is known as the *hidden job market.* Let's examine the hidden job market concept, so that you can appreciate exactly why the networking process is so very successful.

THE HIDDEN JOB MARKET

The hidden job market is a concept that has been around for a long time. There have been a number of employment related articles and books that describe it in various ways; and there is generally a great deal of uniformity about what is said.

It is widely believed, and well supported by both private and independent studies, that a very high percentage of jobs that are filled in the United States are filled informally through personal contact, long before they have had the opportunity to be advertised in a newspaper, or listed with a search firm, or employment agency. In fact, depending on which study you choose to cite, it is believed that between 63.4 and 74.5 percent of all jobs are filled through the informal social networking process. Most authoritative sources place the figure at about 70 percent.

Stated differently, only about 30 percent of all job openings in the United States ever reach the general public and become known through recruitment advertising or employment consultants. This is a rather startling number when we think about the number of persons who rely on advertising and employment agencies as the mainstays of their job hunting process. By restricting themselves to these sources, such persons are missing out on 70 percent of the total job market, right from the start.

If you are in the process of planning your job hunting campaign, it would seem rather foolhardy to ignore a full 70 percent of the market. It is imperative that you pay particular attention to this hidden job market, and that you become intimately familiar with the informal networking process that has been successfully used by so many to access this important segment of the market.

Sometimes people have the impression that this is a market to which only the rich, powerful, or privileged have access. Nothing could be further from the truth. The fact that this segment of the market represents a full 70 percent, should certainly, in itself, convince you otherwise. What makes this a *hidden* job market has nothing to do with access. It simply means that although these jobs exist, they are not readily visible to the general public and, therefore, require a little extra work to flush them out.

The special method that is used to identify and access the jobs that comprise the hidden job market is the informal networking process. Simply put, through personal contact, people become aware of these newly created positions, interview, and are hired to fill them long before they become the subject of a classified ad, display ad, or an employment agency search.

If you are to successfully compete in this important segment of the job market, you must become skilled in the employment networking process. It is this process that provides you the wherewithal to access this valuable market segment. Remember, it represents 70 percent of the job market. It's well worth going after.

The balance of this chapter is designed to train you in the use of the employment networking process. You will walk through this process, step-by-step, and become thoroughly familiar with how it works. If you are an attentive student, this process will serve you extremely well, and will prove to be a major factor in your job search campaign.

RESEARCH PHASE

The first step in the employment networking process is the research phase. The purpose of this phase is twofold:

1. Identification of target companies

2. Identification of Level I contacts

You need to start by identifying the target industry or industries that are likely to have interest in your background, and in which, of course, you would like to be employed. In most cases this should be fairly simple and require little, if any, research.

Next, you will need to consider the geography in which you plan to conduct your search. Will you relocate anywhere in the United States? Will you relocate overseas? Do you have geographical preferences? How about geographical restrictions? These questions need to be answered before you begin listing companies on your target list that are located in geographical areas to which you are unwilling to move. So, carefully define the geographical boundaries of your target area.

Logically, as you have probably already guessed, the next step is to identify the firms within your preferred industry segment and geographical target area, for whom you would like to work. This list of firms becomes your target list.

It is now time to develop your Level I contacts, which will serve to form the nucleus of your networking process. To begin this, make a list of persons whom you know. At this point, don't worry whether they have firsthand knowledge of your target industry or firms. Put each of their names, addresses, and telephone numbers on a three by five index card. Try to generate a list of over 100 of these Level I contacts. To help stimulate your thinking, here is a list of categories from which such contacts could come:

Fellow workers	Salespersons	Consultants
Past bosses	Relatives	Church
Barber	Accountant	Stockbroker
Professional associations	Trade associations	Alumnae associations
Past subordinates	Fraternity	Sorority
Club members	Neighbors	Teachers
Former classmates	Doctor	Dentist
Insurance agent	Lawyer	Banker
Pastor	Priest	Friends
Competitors	Customers	Clients
Military	Government	Editors
Scouting	Sports	Hobbies
Commuting	Grocer	Butcher

Having reviewed these categories and developed as many contact names as possible, sort your index cards into two categories:

1. Those who could potentially know persons in your target industry

2. Those who are less likely to know such persons.

You are now ready to begin the process of contacting these Level I contacts and starting the employment networking process.

MAKING LEVEL I CONTACTS

Level I contacts are, for the most part, persons you know. Although you may at first feel somewhat shy about contacting them and asking for their help, remember the following:

1. Most people really are quite willing to help others, if approached in the right way.

2. Most people feel complimented by a request for advice and counsel. They are frequently pleased that you respect their knowledge enough to seek their counsel.

3. If unemployed, most people will be very understanding. With so many corporations going through downsizing programs, it is no longer a stigma to be unemployed. Additionally, many of the persons with whom you will be talking may have some concerns about their own job security, and are thus quite willing to help. After all, they could well be needing your help at some future point in time.

When contacting these Level I persons, you have the following objectives:

1. Make them aware of your job search.

2. Briefly acquaint them with your background and the type of job you seek.

3. Determine if they are aware of job openings that might be appropriate.

4. If not, ask them to suggest the names of persons who may know of such openings.

5. Determine if they would be willing to arrange a personal introduction to such persons.

6. If not, ask them for permission to use their name when contacting these persons.

7. Ask if they would mind if you send them a copy of your resume. (Objective here is to further acquaint them with your background and make it possible for them to provide a copy of your resume to others).

When calling these contacts, it is very important that you not ask them for a job. You don't want to do anything that would put them on the spot or cause embarrassment. It is best, therefore, to take a more indirect approach. Tell them that you are not asking them for a job, but are simply calling them to ask for assistance and advice in your job hunting campaign. When approached in this manner, most persons are quite willing to help and will do so, provided you give them the opportunity.

Remember, your goal is not only to identify job opportunities, but also to secure the names of referrals who will help expand your networking process. In each case, you should set a goal of acquiring the names of three to five contacts from each personal contact you make. Try to focus these referrals such that they will have contacts in your key target industries, or in the business function in which you have an employment interest.

When garnering the names of new referrals, make sure to transfer this information to an index card immediately. Record not only name, address, and phone number; but also the name of the source of the referral. In addition, if your source was unusually helpful, be sure to send a short *thank you* along with the copy of your resume. Acknowledge your appreciation for his or her assistance in your job hunting campaign.

LEVEL II CONTACTS

Telephone contacts with your Level II Group should be handled somewhat differently from those in the Level I or Primary Group. In all cases, those who you contacted in the Level I or Primary Group were persons you personally know. Those in your Level II Group, however, are persons you have never met or, at best, may have met only briefly. For the most part, these Secondary or Level II contacts will fall into one of two categories:

1. Those either employed or having good personal contacts in your target industry

2. Those not employed or having direct contacts in your target industry.

Those falling into the first of these categories usually warrant a personal meeting, when this can be arranged. Their contacts are particularly valuable and could be extremely helpful to your networking process and overall job hunting campaign. You will want them, if possible, to be a part of your job search campaign, to actively work on your behalf to open doors, to arrange appropriate introductions to key persons within your target firms. There is nothing that can compare to a personal meeting when it comes to getting someone truly involved in helping you with your job hunting campaign. Here are the steps you should follow when trying to set up a meeting by phone:

1. Introduce yourself.

2. Explain that (*name of person making referral*) referred you to him/her and suggested that he/she could be of help to you.

3. Explain that you are not asking for a job, but since he/she is knowledgeable of the industry, you would appreciate the opportunity to meet, in order to get some ideas on how to best approach the industry as far as your job search is concerned.

4. If not possible to arrange a meeting, ask if he/she could take a few moments on the phone to be of some assistance. (Most will agree or, if not convenient, will offer to call back.)

5. Briefly describe your background and job search objective.

6. Ask if he/she is aware of any companies or organizations that may currently be looking for someone with your profile.

7. If so, ask for the names and titles of contacts he/she may have in these companies.

8. Ask if an introduction could be arranged.

9. If no introduction is possible, ask if you may use his/her name in making contact with these persons.

10. If not aware of anyone who is looking for someone with your profile, ask for the names of persons he/she knows who have contacts in this industry and may know persons having such openings. (Try to get the names of three to five such contacts.)

11. Ask if he/she would be willing to arrange a personal introduction.

12. If no personal introduction is possible, ask permission to use this person's name when contacting these referrals.

13. Ask if he/she would mind if you would send him/her a copy of your resume. (Remember to include a thank-you letter along with your resume.)

Should you be successful in arranging a personal meeting with one of these Level II contacts, in addition to the items mentioned above, you should include the following items in your agenda:

1. Ask him/her to review your resume. Ask for thoughts and ideas on how it might be improved. (The objective here is to familiarize others with your background and qualifications).

2. Describe your job hunting strategy. Ask for thoughts and ideas as to how it could be made more effective.

3. Ask for an assessment of the industry. What segments and which companies are expanding? What segments are contracting?

4. What are some of the key issues and challenges currently faced by the industry? How might your background prove helpful?

In all cases, be sure to request the names of additional contacts in the field. This is your lifeline to a successful networking process. Without these key contacts, your campaign will lose its momentum and may eventually stall completely. This is something you can't afford to have happen. So be sure to keep the pipeline flowing with new names.

Contacts with Level III, Level IV, and so on, groups should all be handled in much the same way as described here with the Level II Group.

GENERAL COMMENTS

As you can see, the employment networking process requires considerable time and effort to sustain it. It is a process that requires a great deal of organization and discipline in order to successfully carry it out. There is little question, however, that if you stick with it, the end results will prove well worth the expenditure of time.

Through your persistence and evergrowing network of valuable contacts, sooner or later you will find the position that you are searching for. With 70 percent of the job market at stake, it will definitely be a worthwhile investment of your time and effort.

12

Interview Power: How to Win the Interview

When stepping back from the employment interview process and taking a broader strategic look, there are really two important dimensions for you to consider. They are:

1. Using the interview to package and sell yourself and,

2. Using the interview to measure if a given opportunity is a good career "fit."

It is the purpose of this chapter to teach you various strategies and techniques for effectively selling yourself in the interview. Chapter 13 provides interviewing strategies and techniques to assist you in making a good career decision.

When getting ready for the employment interview, there are quite a number of things that you can do to get ahead of your competition and substantially improve your chances of coming out a winner. Unfortunately, few persons invest the necessary effort to properly prepare for the interview process and the result is often a less than stellar performance.

Most people feel there is little if anything they can do to improve their interviewing skills. Let me assure you, *nothing could be further from the truth!*

If you are willing to invest a small bit of time and effort at the outset, there is much that you can do to dramatically improve your interview effectiveness and positively affect its outcome. There is much you can do, for example, to prepare for the kinds of questions you will be asked by the employer, allowing you to showcase your qualifications and set yourself apart from your competition. Further, there are specific interview strategies you can employ during the interview to clearly stack the deck in your favor. Finally, a little advance research before the interview can go a long way to helping you to come out a winner.

This chapter is designed to help you to systematically plan and execute an interview strategy that will provide you with substantial competitive advantage, and dramatically improve the probability for a successful result.

HOW EMPLOYERS THINK

You can gain important insight, when preparing for the employment interview, by forcing yourself to think as the employer does. Such thinking will allow you to identify those areas on which the employer will most likely focus during the course of the interview.

During the employment interview, the employer's main focus is usually on the candidate's ability to solve key problems and to perform specific job functions. The technical knowledge and skills needed to solve these problems and perform these key functions normally become the central focal point of the job interview. These knowledge and skill factors become the selection criteria against which your qualifications are gauged by the employer during the interview discussion. They comprise the *technical* part of the interview.

It is the technical portion of the interview with which employers are most preoccupied. It is estimated that in the typical interview the average employer will spend 75 to 85 percent of the total interview time exploring the candidate's technical qualifications for the position. This is an important statistic to keep in mind when it comes to interview preparation. It suggests that a similar portion of your interview preparation time should be committed to this same area if you are to be fully prepared to address this core area of focus.

Why is this the case? Why is it that employers spend so much time on technical qualifications rather than other important dimensions of a candidate's overall capability? There are several probable reasons:

1. Technical qualifications are more apparent and, therefore, more easily defined.

2. Technical qualifications are less abstract and are thus more easily measured.

3. Most interviewers are better trained in interviewing for technical qualifications, so are more comfortable in this area.

4. For a manager, there is a tendency to think in terms of the key technical problems that need to be solved. These are the issues foremost in his/her mind.

5. Most managers have had little or no training in techniques for measuring more abstract selection criteria (e.g., motivation or organizational fit). They feel less comfortable in these areas, therefore, and will tend to shy away or de-emphasize such categories.

Although devoting considerably less time to this category, the second major area on which employers will focus during the employment interview is the area of employee motivation. Unlike technical credentials, which are the *can-do* aspect of a candidate's qualifications, the motivation area is the *will-do* dimension of selection. A candidate may be technically qualified and able to perform the job, but is he or she sufficiently interested and motivated to actually do the job (or to do it well)? Most employers understand this subtle difference and attempt to gain some insight into the candidate's motivation to do the job during the interview discussion.

Because of the abstract nature of motivation, most interviewers will make some basic observations about the candidate in this area, but will not commit much interview time to doing so. Fundamental questions about the candidate's interest in the position and general work ethic may surface during the interview, but few interviewers are adequately prepared to probe this area much more deeply than this. It is estimated that only about 10 to 15 percent of total interview time is committed to investigating the motivational or can-do factors.

Although employers seldom think of it in these terms, the final area of employer focus during the employment interview is organizational compatibility (i.e., how well the individual will fit into the organization's culture). Again, due to the abstract nature of this concept, attempts by the employer to measure organizational compatibility are, for the most part, fairly shallow and seem to center around a rather vague notion of liking or not liking the candidate.

Although clearly an important factor in effective interviewing and employee selection, the notion of organizational compatibility is an area where most interviewers feel least prepared to measure a candidate's qualifications through specific interview techniques. Simply put, most employers don't really know what kind of questions to ask in order to examine this important area more thoroughly. As a consequence, very little interview time is ever committed to asking questions concerning organizational compatibility (probably less than five percent). As a candidate, however, it is important to be aware that although employers may invest little if any direct interview time in exploring this area specifically, you can be sure than employers will, nonetheless, make some very real (if not potentially inaccurate) observations about your ability to "fit in."

Thus, in order for you to properly prepare for the interview and enhance your chances for coming out a winner, you will need to prepare yourself to address the following three critical areas.

1. Technical qualifications (The can-do factors)

2. Motivational qualifications (The will-do factors)

3. Organizational compatibility.

This is exactly where you can expect the employer to focus during interview discussions, and it is therefore important to your interview success to be well prepared in these three areas.

Knowing that the employer will concentrate on these three dimensions, how can you prepare in advance of the interview to effectively address these focal points? What sort of questions should you anticipate being asked, and how can you be ready to answer them?

The next few pages of this chapter systematically explore each of these interview areas so that you can anticipate how the employer will approach them and know what to expect. Furthermore, you will be provided with specific strategies and techniques for greatly improving your interview effectiveness in each of these important areas.

TECHNICAL QUALIFICATIONS

How does one go about determining the technical qualifications for a given position in advance of the interview? The logical answer to this is, "Through some thoughtful position analysis." Consider, for a moment, the thought process that the employer typically goes through when defining the technical requirements of the position.

Typically, when an employer begins the process of developing selection criteria (i.e., the "candidate specification") for use in the interview, the first step is to review certain key factors relating to both the position as well as the department in which the position is located. This usually includes such things as the job description, department business plan, department objectives, and specific business objectives.

While reviewing these factors, the employer attempts to determine the key functions and responsibilities of the position, and then translates those into those technical qualifications felt to be essential to good job performance.

Although you may not have all of these factors available to you, in most cases it is at least possible to secure a copy of the job description from the employer in advance of an interview. Most employers will be willing to provide a copy of this document to you if you only ask for it. Once you have obtained a copy of the job description, you are in a position to go through the same type of position analysis that the employer will likely go through in translating the requirements of the position into a candidate specification. The following questions will help you to conduct a fairly complete analysis of the position.

1. What are the key functions for which this position is accountable?

   _____

   _____

   _____

   _____

2. Which of these functions are most important to job success?

   _____

   _____

   _____

3. In which of these functions is it essential that the candidate have experience? How much and what kind?

_____

_____

_____

_____

_____

4. What are the principal, ongoing responsibilities of this position (i.e., the ongoing results expected of the job)?

_____

_____

_____

_____

5. What technical knowledge and skills are needed by the candidate to achieve these required results on an ongoing basis?

_____

_____

_____

_____

6. What are the key technical issues and problems to be solved by the incumbent in this position?

_____

_____

_____

_____

7. What technical knowledge and skills must a candidate have to successfully solve these problems and address these issues?

_____

_____

_____

_____

_____

8. What level and type of formal education is likely required to equip a candidate to successfully handle the technical aspects of this position?

_____

_____

_____

_____

_____

As with the employer, by answering these or similar questions, you should be able to delineate a list of technical or can-do qualifications important to successful job performance. These qualifications can normally be classified into the following categories:

Formal Education

> The level and type of formal education needed for successful performance

Functional Experience

> The level and type of experience required in specific functional areas

Technical Capability

The technical knowledge and skills needed to solve the key problems and meet the major technical challenges of the position.

SELF-EVALUATION

Modern interview theory is based upon the concept that the best predictor of future behavior is past behavior. To put it differently, if you want to forecast how well a person will do carrying out a certain function or solving a certain kind of problem, find out how well he or she did tackling similar things in the past. If results were good in the past, there is some basis for believing that they will be equally as good in the future. This type of behavioral interviewing is becoming very popular today and is in fairly widespread use.

In order to prepare for a behavioral interview (which, by the way, is an excellent way to prepare for almost any type interview), you will need to systematically analyze your past experience in search of evidence that you have, (and can apply), the technical knowledge and skills that are required for successful performance of your desired position. It is no longer enough to simply state that you meet these requirements; you must be prepared to demonstrate this from the results you have achieved in the past. The closer these examples are to current issues and problems faced by the employer, the more convinced the employer will be that you have the necessary skills and technical capability to perform well in the position for which you will be interviewing.

In order to simplify this process and save considerable time, refer to the historical information that you prepared from Chapter 5 of this book. You will recall that, in assembling this data, you were required to furnish a list of responsibilities and accomplishments for each of your past positions. This information is an excellent basis for systematically reviewing your past background for evidence of the technical knowledge and skills currently sought by the interviewer. The questions listed below should prove helpful in sifting out relevant information as you go along.

One of the advantages to using this approach is that this same information served as the basis for preparing your resume. So, much of this information is probably already contained in your resume, and the interviewer's attention can be drawn to this fact as the interview progresses.

Key Questions for Self-Evaluation

1. In which of your past positions were you accountable for the same (or similar) functional areas as required for this position?

_____

_____

_____

_____

2. What functions were they, and what was the nature of your accountability?

_____

_____

_____

_____

3. With which of these required functions have you had little or no experience?

_____

_____

_____

4. In such cases, what (if any) experience have you had in related functional areas that might be considered equivalent experience?

_____

_____

_____

_____

5. In which of your past positions have you had the same or similar principal, ongoing responsibilities as required by this position?

_____

_____

_____

_____

6. What were the key technical problems that you were required to solve in order to meet these principal, ongoing responsibilities?

_____

_____

_____

_____

7. How well did you do? What key problems were solved? What important results were achieved?

Key Problems: _____

_____

_____

Important Results: _____

_____

_____

_____

8. What key technical problems and issues did you face in past jobs that were the same (or similar) to the issues and problems you will face in the new position?

_____

_____

_____

_____

9. How well did you do? What key problems or issues did you resolve? What important results did you achieve?

Key Problems: _____

_____

_____

Important Results: _____

_____

_____

10. In what ways do these results demonstrate the technical knowledge and skills sought by the prospective employer?

_____

_____

_____

_____

11. What does this analysis tell you about your overall qualifications to successfully meet the technical challenges of the new position?

_____

_____

_____

12. What relevant major problems are you likely to be able to solve for your new employer? With what probable results?

Relevant Problems: _____

_____

_____

Probable Results: _____

_____

_____

13. What evidence can you cite to substantiate this capability?

_____

_____

_____

_____

14. Where are your shortfalls? What key technical problems are you likely not to be able to solve in the new position?

_____

_____

_____

_____

15. What specific technical knowledge or skills do you lack that would account for this lack of capability?

_____

_____

_____

_____

16. What steps are you prepared to take in order to acquire this knowledge or skills?

_____

_____

_____

_____

17. How will you manage this part of the job while you acquire the needed capability?

_____

_____

_____

_____

As you can see, working diligently to answer these questions is an excellent way to prepare you for the forthcoming interview. It focuses your attention on those aspects of the job most likely to be of interest to the prospective employer. In addition, it prepares you to quickly cite convincing evidence of your overall ability to perform key elements of the job.

This exercise thoroughly prepares you to discuss specific knowledge and skills necessary to good job performance and to also cite behavioral evidence that objectively supports your professional competence in these critical areas. Such vigorous preparation will clearly improve your interview results and provide you with a substantial competitive advantage over other candidates with whom you will need to compete for the position.

MOTIVATIONAL QUALIFICATIONS

As previously stated in this chapter, motivational qualifications are certain personal traits and characteristics necessary to achieve the key results required for good job performance. It is the drive, energy, and desire to accomplish these results. It is one thing to simply have the technical qualifications to perform the responsibilities of the job. It is quite another to be motivated to actually do the work. Without such motivation, key results will likely not be achieved and there will be a high probability of performance failure. Employers are generally aware of this and tend to look for signs of good motivation during the interview.

When attempting to measure these motivational factors, employers will normally ask certain questions and then observe candidate behavior, looking for signs of interest or disinterest. Seasoned interviewers will be particularly alert to the candidate's body language, which can often telegraph the candidate's interest in (motivation to perform) the work.

Here are some key questions that the employer may use to assess your interest and motivation to perform the job:

1. How do you feel about this position?

2. What aspect of the job most interests you?

3. What aspect of the job least interests you? Why?

4. How would you rate your overall interest in this position? Why?

5. Which of your past positions did you like most? Why?

6. Which of your past positions did you like least? Why?

7. Which of these past positions most resembles this new position? In what ways?

8. What factors must be present to make a job interesting and exciting for you?

9. What factors would make a job less interesting and exciting?

10. Which of these factors are present in this job?

11. What aspects of this job are you likely to perform best? Why?

12. What aspects of this job are you likely to perform least well? Why?

13. On a scale of one to ten (ten, high), where would you rate the level of your interest in this position?

14. How might you change this job to make it more interesting and exciting?

15. What concerns do you have about this job? Why?

In addition to being prepared to answer these questions in a way that clearly demonstrates a high level of interest in the position for which you are interviewing, you also need to pay particular attention to your body language during the interview. For maximum effectiveness, you want to appear alert, interested, and relatively enthusiastic throughout the interview process. Here are some clues about body language that should help you to accomplish this.

1. Sit up relatively straight (but not rigid) in your chair. Good posture can convey a feeling of positive energy and an increased level of interest in the conversation. It can also suggest that you are a person who is alert, attentive, and interested in the ideas of others.

2. Never lay back or slouch in your chair. This may suggest that you are lazy, sloppy, careless, inattentive, or disinterested.

3. Acknowledge key points made by your host with nod, smile, or other appropriate gesture that suggests you are attentive and responsive to the conversational topic.

4. Good eye contact with the interviewer is important throughout the interview. In addition to telegraphing your attentiveness, eye contact conveys that you are sensitive, open, forthright, secure, self-confident, and comfortable in your relationship with others.

5. To the contrary, poor eye contact may suggest that you are inattentive, disinterested, shifty, uncertain, unsure, self-conscious, shy, and ill-at-ease in your interpersonal relations.

6. Avoid nervous habits such as tapping your pencil or fingers, pulling your ear lobes, rubbing your nose, playing with your tie, stroking your hair. These habits can be annoying and detract from your presentation. In addition, such actions suggest that you are nervous, high-strung, intense, insecure, and generally uncomfortable with others.

7. Avoid crossing your arms in front of you. To some, this may indicate that you are defensive, unfriendly, and prefer to keep others at a distance.

Body language can, and does, have a very real impact on interview results. In particular, it can transmit strong messages to the employer concerning your motivation, drive, energy, desire, and general interest level. Seasoned interviewers will closely observe your behavior and body language throughout the interview discussion for signs of your level of interest and motivation to perform the job. You will therefore want to exhibit positive body language throughout the interview.

During the interview, you should also be alert for opportunities to demonstrate your motivation and confirm you interest in the position. Be sure to verbally express your interest and demonstrate your enthusiasm as the opportunity presents itself. Here are a few statements and phrases that can help accomplish this:

1. That sounds very interesting!

2. I have always particularly liked doing _____!

3. That sounds exciting and challenging!

4. I think I could do that quite well!

5. That's an area where I feel I could make some meaningful contributions.

6. I have some ideas on how to approach that issue.

7. Here's how I would approach that.

8. I feel that kind of work is challenging and exciting!

9. I've always been fascinated by _____.

10. I would enjoy doing that!

11. That sounds challenging and stimulating!

12. I have always had a strong interest in _____.

13. I feel I could make some real contributions to _____.

14. I would welcome the challenge of doing _____.

15. That's an exciting area—one that is continually challenging and interesting to me.

Don't pass up the opportunity to express your interest and desire for the position at the conclusion of the interview. If you are really interested in the job, tell your host of your interest. Tell him or her that you have enjoyed your interview, and that it has served to heighten your interest in the position. Briefly summarize key areas of the job that sound particularly attractive. Voice your confidence that you can perform well in the position, and that you have a strong interest. Here is an example of something you might say:

> Mr. Jones, I have enjoyed the day. Although I was already interested in this position, today's discussions have heightened this interest. I would enjoy doing _____, _____ and _____; and feel these are areas where I could make a strong contribution to the ABC Company. In many ways, this position seems like a good fit for my experience, skills, and capabilities. I hope the ABC Company will elect to pursue this further. I look forward to hearing from you.

Thus, by demonstrating your interest and enthusiasm for the position, both verbally and through body language, you suggest to the employer that you are well-motivated to perform successfully in the job. Interest and enthusiasm convey that you have the necessary drive, energy, and desire to accomplish the objectives and results. You satisfy not only the technical or can-do requirements of the position, but also the motivational or will-do requirements, as well. This leaves only the matter of organizational compatibility.

ORGANIZATIONAL COMPATIBILITY

As mentioned earlier in this chapter, employers are usually not well versed in measuring this factor. They will, nevertheless, make some judgments about your organizational compatibility. How well do your ideas and philosophy align with that of the organization? How well do your style and personality fit with the other members of the group with whom you will be working? These are concerns that will be on the employer's mind, and you will want to be aware of this as you prepare for your interview discussion.

Interviewers who are more seasoned and skillful than others may attempt to probe this area. If they do, here are some of the questions that you might anticipate:

1. How would you describe yourself? What adjectives would you use?

2. How have your past bosses described you? What have they said when describing you?

3. How would you describe your operating style? What is characteristic about the way in which you operate?

4. How would you describe the type of environment in which you enjoy working? What is characteristic of that environment?

5. Of the various environments in which you have worked, which did you most enjoy? Why? What was present in that environment?

6. Of the various environments in which you have worked, which did you least enjoy? Why? What was present that accounted for your dissatisfaction?

7. What is your business philosophy? What do you believe is important to having a successful operation?

8. What type of business philosophy do you find least agreeable? What do you feel makes such a philosophy less effective?

9. With what kind of people do you most enjoy working? What is characteristic about such people?

10. How would you categorize the kind of people with whom you least enjoy associating?

Other than being aware of these potential questions and thinking about how you will want to respond to them, there is probably very little that you can do to prepare for this area. At the time of the interview, however, there are some things that you can do, in a strategic sense, to stack the deck somewhat in your favor. Here are a few pointers:

1. During the interview, be particularly alert to the environment around you.

2. Make careful observations about the kind of people that you meet.

3. In what ways are these people similar?

4. In what ways are they different?

5. What observations can you make about their personal styles?

6. Are there some common attributes (e.g., conservative, liberal, risk-taking, entrepreneurial, careful, analytical)?

7. What observations can you make about their operating styles? Are there some general conformities?

8. What is the overriding management style and philosophy?

9. What is characteristic about the leaders of the group?

10. In what ways are these leaders similar (i.e., personality, operating style, philosophy)?

11. In what ways are they different (i.e., personal characteristics, operating style, business philosophy)?

Observations of this type can prove very helpful in understanding the organizational culture and environment. The data that you collect through this process can be very helpful in guiding your answers to the questions that the employer may ask, as outlined previously. For example, if your observations suggest that this is a very conservative, analytical group that values good planning and analytical skills, you don't want to come across as a highly creative risk-taker, who likes to make quick decisions an get on with the action. Clearly, you would be a mismatch and would not be seen as compatible with the group. Nothing will scuttle you chances faster!

A word of caution, however. Although these strategies may improve your competitive edge in winning the interview, it may not be the best thing for your career. It would be irresponsible of me not to draw this to your attention. What good is it to win the interview if the end result is going to require you to work in an environment in which you will be unhappy? Sooner or later, this unhappiness will result in your personal isolation and reflect in your performance. This issue will be more deeply discussed in the next chapter, where we discuss some methods for examining the matter of organizational fit.

If you are incompatible with the culture and organizational environment of the company with which you are interviewing, move on to your next target company and next set of interviews as soon as possible. Why risk unhappiness, and possibly your career, when the odds are decidedly against you?

We have not thoroughly covered the topics of technical qualifications (the can-do factors), motivation (the will-do factors), and organizational compatibility (organizational fit). You have been given a step-by-step process and methodology for thoroughly preparing yourself for these three important areas of the job interview. If you have invested the necessary time and effort in these exercises, you will have substantially improved your interview skills and readiness, and assured yourself of a strong competitive advantage in the interview process. Few, if any candidates, will be better prepared for this important test.

Beyond preparing yourself to address the three areas we have just discussed, there are some additional things you can do to strengthen your competitive position in the interview. The balance of this chapter is devoted to discussion of some strategies that can further serve to strengthen your overall interview effectiveness.

ADVANCE KNOWLEDGE— CANDIDATE SPECIFICATION

The term *candidate specification* is used by employment professionals to describe the document that is prepared by the employer to describe the qualifications needed for successful performance in the position. This candidate specification normally consists of a list of specific knowledge, skills, and experience that the employer feels are essential to successful performance of the technical aspects of the job. It may also describe the personal style and attributes thought to be important to job success. In most companies, this specification is typically reduced to writing, and is passed along to both the employment department, as well as the members of the interview team, who will be involved in the interview and selection process.

Having access to this candidate specification in advance of the interview is analogous to having a copy of the final exam in advance of the test date. It gives you an opportunity to study and prepare, thus substantially improving the probability of doing well and achieving high marks. Knowing the contents of this candidate specification in advance will provide you with a bird's-eye view of what is important to the employer and, therefore, what topics are most likely to become the focal points of the interview process. This will allow you to anticipate the kinds of questions you are likely to be asked, and will substantially improve the probability of a favorable outcome.

So, what can you do to secure this information in advance of the interview? The answer is simple—*just ask for it!* You shouldn't expect that someone will give you a written copy; instead, ask for a verbal description of these requirements.

Strategically speaking, the best time to ask for a description of the candidate specification is at the time you are first contacted by the employer. It is at this time that the balance of power is in your favor, and you have the greatest leverage to extract this vital information from the employer. Since, at this point, the employer is intent on selling you on the idea of an employment interview, you are in the unique position to extract some key information which, at other times, may be more difficult to secure. To make the most of this opportunity, it is suggested that you might wish to employ the following approach:

1. Tell the employer that, although the position sounds somewhat interesting, you would appreciate a little more information to help you decide whether the position would be an optimal match for your qualifications and interest.

2. Ask for a description of the key functional responsibilities of the position (preferably written, if one is available).

3. What are the key problems and challenges that the company will want someone in this position to address?

4. In what areas is the company looking for major improvement?

5. What is the company looking for in a candidate?

6. What in your background caught their eye?

7. Assuming you are interested at this point, thank the employer for the information and say that you would like to accept the interview invitation.

Be careful not to push for too much information at this point, since this strategy could backfire. If the employer begins to stiffen and you sense that you are either pushing too hard or are simply asking for too much, back off. Continuing to push for more information could work to your disadvantage by implying that you are too pushy, overly cautious, indecisive, or lacking in self-confidence.

If you are successful in your endeavor, however, you have pulled off an important strategic coup. Since you now have a thorough understanding of the employer's requirements and priorities, you are in an excellent position to know what aspects of your background and qualifications are likely to be of greatest interest.

Strategically, this provides you with considerable advantage over potential competition by allowing you to emphasize and showcase those skills and abilities of greatest interest to the employer.

THE "PERFORMANCE IMPROVEMENT" STRATEGY

The basic objective of the performance improvement strategy is for you to establish yourself as someone who can solve the ongoing problems faced by the employer, and thus bring about improved organizational performance. In my book, *The Five Minute Interview,* I refer to this as the *voids* strategy.

In order to employ this strategy, you must first determine performance voids in the current organization. What aspects of the current position, in the opinion of the hiring manager (the one to whom you would report), could be better performed? This, and similar questions, need to be answered during the early stages of the interview discussion so that you will be able to have time to think and carefully formulate a strategy that will allow you to position yourself as someone who can effectively address these deficits and contribute to the improved effectiveness of the organization.

Here are the types of questions that you can employ early in the interview to identify these employment voids, and to quickly hone in on areas where the employer desires improvement:

1. In your judgment, what areas of the current job could be better performed?

2. What kind of improvement would you like to see in these areas? Why?

3. In which of these areas would you most like to see improvement?

4. Why is improvement in this key area of particular interest to you?

5. What kind of improvement would you like to see in this key area?

6. Are there key, ongoing responsibilities of this position not currently being met? What are they?

7. Which of these, if any, do you feel are important? Why?

8. What factors have hindered performance of these responsibilities? Why?

9. What major changes and improvements would you most like to see brought about by a new incumbent? Why?

10. What type of improvement would you like to see?

11. What major barriers and obstacles stand in the way of realizing this improvement?

Answers to these questions will provide you with some ideas of the kinds of changes and improvements that the new boss would like to see brought to the organization. By demonstrating your willingness and ability to tackle these areas, and by citing evidence of similar problems you have successfully tackled in the past, you will position yourself as someone who will bring change and improvement to the organization. Most importantly, such improvement is in areas the hiring manager personally considers essential to organization effectiveness.

If carefully executed, this can prove to be an effective strategy. It creates the impression that you are someone who is focused on bringing change and improvement to the organization. In this sense, it suggests that you are someone who is willing to go beyond the traditional boundaries of the job, someone who will reach out in an effort to add value to the organization.

THE "STRATEGIC CHANGE AGENT" STRATEGY

Another key strategy that you can employ to increase your interview effectiveness is to position yourself as a *strategic change agent*—one who can help the organization to drive forward in the achievement of its strategic goals and mission.

Although always in demand, the popularity and desire to hire strategic change agents has grown dramatically. In the last few years, with intensified competition from foreign competition, many U.S. firms and industries have been operating in a survival mode. The intensity of competition is forcing organizations to accelerate change at a rate that has never before been seen. Corporations are beginning to set very high goals for major improvement and are wanting to bring these improvements about on an immediate basis. The acceleration and intensity of international competition have raised concerns about continued growth and long-term economic survival.

These changes have had significant impact on the interview and selection process. Generally, most employers are now looking for candidates who have a proclivity to strategic change. They no longer need people who can come in and simply perform the job. Instead, they are looking for those who will change the job, those who will reach out and push the barriers of traditional job performance, those who will bring productive change and improvement, those who will be "value adding" to the organization.

The key to this "strategic change interview strategy" is knowing what change it is that the employer wishes to bring about. Effective implementation of this strategy therefore requires that you have a good understanding of the strategic goals and objectives of the organization. Here are some good questions to use at the beginning of the interview to flush this important information out:

1. What are the overall strategic goals and objectives of the organization?

2. What are the major strategic changes that the organization wishes to bring about?

3. What effect will these changes have on the department or function for which I will be working?

4. What new results will be expected?

5. Considering these strategic changes, what new skills and capabilities will be necessary to ensure successful job performance in the future?

6. Which of these qualifications will be most important? Why?

You will note that these questions have been designed to help the job candidate to define not only the key strategic changes that the employer desires, but also to define the important skills and capabilities that the employer feels are vital to future performance success.

As with the performance improvement strategy previously discussed, these questions should be asked early in the interview discussion so that you will be able to have time to think and formulate your interview strategy. To be effective, this strategy will require that you emphasize those skills and capabilities required to drive strategic change, and realize the strategic goals and objectives of the company. You need to position yourself, therefore, as someone who can drive these changes, realize the desired results and add strategic value to the organization. This establishes you as someone who is capable of going considerably beyond the traditional boundaries of the current job, someone who will drive positive change, someone who is truly capable of adding significant value to the organization, someone who will provide the company with the ability to achieve its future objectives and accomplish its strategic mission.

THE "IDEAL CANDIDATE" STRATEGY

A final strategy that you might successfully use to gain a very real competitive advantage in the employment interview is what I call the "ideal candidate" strategy. As with the other two strategies we have discussed, this strategy is best applied early in the interview if you are to realize maximum mileage from its use.

When using this strategy, you will simply want to ask the employer (and even more importantly, the hiring manager to whom you would report) to describe the "ideal candidate" for the position. Here is how you might wish to word this inquiry

> Joan, how would you describe the ideal candidate for this position? What are you really looking for in a candidate?

As you can see, by gaining this insight early in the interview you have provided yourself with an enormous advantage. In short, you have succeeded in determining exactly what Joan is buying—that is, what specific knowledge, skills and attributes will most motivate her to want to hire a particular candidate. You now know what specific qualifications she is most interested in.

Top sales producers have always been aware of this approach as being an extremely powerful technique in sales success. It is referred to as "qualifying the buyer," and it is one of the first things an effective sales representative will do when making a sales presentation.

The underlying idea is that you must discover, early in the sales presentation, which of the many product attributes are going to be most important to the buyer's purchasing decision. Although the product may have many attributes, only certain of these will be the ones that will actually motivate this person to buy. By focusing on these particular attributes (i.e., those that motivate to buy versus those that are unimportant to the buying decision), the sales representative gets right to the heart of the matter and substantially increases the probability of making the sale.

Conversely, ineffective sales representatives fail to "qualify the buyer." Not knowing what is important to the buyer from the onset, they frequently waste valuable time discussing all of the product's attributes—many of which are of little or no interest. Even worse, they may neglect to mention those product attributes that the buyer considers most important. The end result—"no sale"!

This analogy has direct application to interviewing strategy. If you are going to win in the interview (i.e., make the sale, so to speak), you need to know what the employer is really buying. The "ideal candidate" strategy allows you to do just that! By determining what candidate qualifications (i.e., product attributes) are going to be most important to the hiring (i.e., buying) decision, you will have an opportunity to focus on these and substantially increase the probability of getting an employment offer (i.e., making the sale).

One minor word of caution about this strategy. It is likely to work best with those who are inexperienced interviewers. If used on the seasoned, professional interviewer, the "ideal candidate" strategy will likely elicit a response similar to the following:

> Joan, although that is certainly a good question I wouldn't wish to bias our discussion by answering it at this stage of the interview. Perhaps we can return to this item later in our discussion, at which time I would be pleased to provide you with an answer, Right now, however, I think we should spend some time getting to know you better.

This is obviously a polite rebuff, and it would not benefit you to continue to pursue this matter at this particular point. Should you be initially rebuffed, however, don't be reluctant to return to this strategy toward the end of the interview discussion. Remember the old adage—*Nothing ventured, nothing gained!* If your host answers your question, you at least still have a few minutes remaining in the discussion to focus on these areas and make the sale.

Before leaving this topic, let me assure you that the majority of persons you encounter during the interview process will not be seasoned, trained interviewers. In fact, I would estimate that upwards of 80 percent or more of the interviewers you encounter during the course of your job search will have had only limited professional interview training. Thus, the great majority will respond positively to the "ideal candidate" strategy—and provide

you with the information requested. So, my advice to you is—
"Go for it!"

COMMON INTERVIEW QUESTIONS

You have now been exposed to several key interviewing strategies that can provide immeasurable assistance to your overall
effectiveness in the interview process. Being prepared with
these interviewing strategies alone, however, will not guarantee
a positive interview result. Additionally, you will need to be
prepared to effectively answer a wide variety of penetrating
questions that are likely to be asked during the interview, if you
are to emerge a clear winner from the interview process.

It would be impossible for any book to list all of the questions that could possibly be asked in the course of an employment
interview. The array of possible choices is just too enormous.
There are too many variables (e.g., organizations, industries,
occupations, skills) to make this a practical consideration. It is
only possible, therefore, to select a sampling of interview questions that are felt to be representative of the kinds that you are
likely to encounter. The following questions, in addition to being
fairly common, are also among the more difficult and thought-
provoking. They should prove a good warm up exercise for helping to fine tune your interviewing skills.

Early Background

These are representative of the questions that might be asked
concerning your childhood and family background:

1. Tell me about your early childhood.

2. What major events occurred during your childhood that
   had the greatest impact on your life?

3. In what ways did these help to shape your life?

4. How would you describe your early family life?

5. What important values did you acquire during your early years?

6. How have these affected your life?

7. Who most influenced you during your early years?

8. What impact did this person have on you?

9. What do you consider to be your most significant accomplishments while growing up?

10. Why were they significant?

Education

1. What were your reasons for choosing _____ college?

2. What were the factors that led to your decision to select _____ as a major?

3. How did your college education prepare you for life?

4. How did your college education prepare you for your current career?

5. What were your most significant accomplishments in college?

6. Why were they significant?

7. What kind of a student were you?

8. How might you have improved your effectiveness as a student?

9. What were your favorite courses? Why?

10. Which courses did you like least? Why?

11. How did you make use of your spare time?

12. What leadership roles did you assume while on campus?

13. How effective were you as a leader?

14. What results demonstrate your effectiveness as a leader?

15. What did you learn as a leader?

Work Experience

1. How did you decide to select _____ as a career?

2. What were the factors that most influenced this decision?

3. Of the past positions that you have held, which did you like most? Why?

4. Which past position did you like least? Why?

5. What were the factors that led to your decision to join _____ company?

6. What were the events and factors that led to your departure from _____ company?

7. What were your most important contributions and accomplishments in your position as _____ with _____ company?

8. How would you compare your position as _____ with _____ company to your position as _____ with _____ company?

9. Which of these positions did you like most? Why?

10. Which of these positions did you enjoy least? Why?

11. If we were to contact your current boss for a reference, what would he say about you?

12. What would he describe as your strengths? Why?

13. What areas would be identified as needing improvement? Why?

14. What are you doing to improve these areas?

15. What could you do to improve your overall performance in your current position?

16. What do you like most about your current job? Why?

17. What do you like least about your current job? Why?

18. What major projects have you undertaken in your current job that are beyond those normally required for this position?

19. How satisfied have you been with your career progress to date?

20. What could you have done to accelerate this progress?

21. Why didn't you do this?

Personal Effectiveness

1. How would you describe yourself?

2. What kind of adjectives would others use to describe you?

3. What are your strengths?

4. In what areas do you need improvement?

5. What are you doing to improve in these areas?

6. How have your past supervisors described you?

7. What have historically been cited as your major strengths?

8. What have historically been cited as areas in which you need to improve? Why?

9. What major changes and improvements have you brought in your last job?

10. Why were these important?

11. How could you have been more effective in your past job?

12. What additional things could you have done to improve your overall impact and performance?

13. Why didn't you do these things?

14. Tell me about your last performance evaluation.

15. What was your last performance rating? Why?

16. If I were to contact each of your past bosses, what would they tell me about your past performance?

17. What plans do you have for improving your effectiveness?

18. In your last job, beyond your normal job responsibilities, what additional major projects did you undertake?

19. How did these extra projects come about?

20. What were the results?

21. In your career to date, what do you consider to be your most significant accomplishment? Why?

22. What was your second most important accomplishment?

23. Why was this important?

24. What is the single most important thing that you could do to improve your overall effectiveness?

Managerial Leadership

1. How would you describe your management style?

2. What are the methods and techniques that you employ when managing others?

3. How effective are these?

4. What results have you gotten?

5. How would your subordinates describe you as a manager?

6. In what areas would they be complimentary?

7. What areas would they likely cite as areas in which you could improve your effectivenss as a manager?

8. What would they say about these areas? Why?

9. How would you describe your management philosophy?

10. What do you see as the major role of management? Why?

11. What is the proper balance between managerial control and employee independence?

12. How do you motivate employees? What kinds of things do you do?

13. What methods do you use to monitor and direct department results?

14. How do you deal with employee performance issues?

15. What methods do you use?

16. Describe your management planning process.

17. How do you go about planning for department results?

18. Who is involved in your planning process?

19. In what ways do you involve them?

20. On a scale of one to ten (ten, high), where would you rate yourself as a manager? Why?

21. How could you improve your overall managerial effectiveness?

This concludes the chapter on interviewing. You should now agree that there is much you can do to dramatically refine your interviewing skills and readiness. With a little patience, good planning, and hard work, it is quite possible to substantially improve your interview effectiveness, and assure a very real competitive advantage in the interview process.

Being an interviewee who can skillfully market his/her overall capability, is one thing; being adept at evaluating the interviewer, is quite another. This is the subject of the next chapter.

13

Making the "Right" Employment Decision

We are now at the most critical step of the job search process—selecting the right job and employer. The goal of any successful job search process, as we discussed in Chapter 2 of this book, is not simply to find a job, but to find job/career satisfaction and happiness. Life is too short, and we spend entirely too much of our time either at work or engaged in work-related activities not to enjoy what we are doing.

If you think about it, most professionals and managers spend an estimated 50 to 60 hours a week in work-related activities. Considering that people sleep an average of 8 hours per day, this means that they are awake an average of 112 hours per week, thus, work related activities occupy more than 50 percent of your waking hours. If you don't like your boss, the work that you do, or the environment in which you work, this means that you are spending nearly half of your conscious lives in a state of dissatisfaction and unhappiness.

Unfortunately, work-related unhappiness is not simply left behind at the workplace at the end of the day, waiting behind a closed door until you return the next day. Instead, it goes right along home with you and has a way of spilling over into your personal life, coloring much of your outlook, and affecting the way you feel about yourself and how you behave toward others.

Not only does quality of worklife affect your state-of-mind, but it has physical implications as well. Much has been written on the topic the relationship between mental attitude and physical well-being. Studies have proven that job-related stress and anxiety can have dire consequences from a health standpoint and, in many cases, can be a key contributor to chronic illnesses resulting in death.

Yes, you can pay a very, very dear price for making a poor employment decision. The sad thing is that much of this unhappiness, and related subsequent problems, can be avoided with a little self-discipline and some careful attention to the process that you use in arriving at your employment decision. That is what this chapter is about.

This chapter will help you to evaluate more objectively employment opportunities through use of a "predictive modeling" process. Wise and judicious use of this process should prepare you to make an intelligent, informed employment decision based not simply on job content, but focusing instead on those factors that are important to your job satisfaction and overall career satisfaction.

THE PREDICTIVE MODEL

It is now time to review the results of all of the hard work that you did back in Chapter 2 when constructing your own predictive model. You will recall, that you went through a series of self-assessment exercises resulting in a comprehensive model that accurately depicts those job, boss and organizational attributes that are known to be very important to both your performance success as well as your happiness. It is precisely this "predictive model" that needs to be used as the basis for evaluating prospective employment opportunities and arriving at an objective, intelligent employment decision.

As you may recall, when stripped down to its basics, the personal predictive model that you have constructed was designed to help you to measure four things:

1. Job Fit

2. Compatibility with Organizational Culture

4. Compatibility with Business Strategy

3. Compatibility with Boss.

Each of these components are absolutely critical to job/career success and happiness.

To complete the job selection process intelligently, it makes logical sense that you will need to systematically examine these same four components with respect to employers and specific job opportunities that you are considering. When evaluating a given employment opportunity, therefore, you will need to systematically collect data about each of these four areas so that you will have the information that you will eventually need to make an informed choice.

If well-planned and executed, the predictive model process will allow you to construct a valid job and "organizational model" of the target opportunity that you are considering and predict, with a high degree of accuracy, whether or not this organizational model is a good match for your own "personal predictive model." In this way, you can take a lot of the guesswork out of the employment selection process and ensure that you are making your employment decision on the basis of those factors that are known to be important to your own personal job/career success and satisfaction.

Let's now examine each of these four selection components and the steps that you will need to take in order to formulate and construct a valid job and organizational model to be used as the basis for this important comparison. The result of this process will be the construction of an "organizational model" against which you can compare your personal "predictive model" for purposes of arriving at a well-founded employment decision.

JOB FIT

The question of "job fit" has to do with whether or not you have the technical knowledge/skills and motivation to actually perform the job. In examining this important organizational profiling component, there are two critical factors to examine. These are:

1. Core Knowledge and Skills

2. Motivation to Perform.

Having the core knowledge and skills to perform the job is one thing, being motivated to perform is yet another. Both of these elements must be firmly in place if there is to be a reasonable expectation for performance success and job satisfaction. We will now address each of these elements and provide you with some practical exercises that should be helpful in accurately constructing the job profile.

Before proceeding with the following exercises, take a plain piece of white paper and draw a large circle. Label this circle "Job Profile." Once you have completed these exercises, you will be transferring certain descriptive information about the job and work environment to this sheet, thus constructing the first part of the "organizational profile."

It should be pointed out that you will generally not have the information needed to complete these exercises until after the employment interview has taken place. You will want to review these exercises in advance of the interview, therefore, so that you will have the opportunity to probe each of these key areas quite thoroughly during the course of the interview itself.

PROFILING CORE JOB KNOWLEDGE

It should stand to reason that the first aspect of the target job that you will need to evaluate is the core knowledge needed to successfully perform the position. Core knowledge means the specialized or technical knowledge necessary for you to successfully solve the key problems that you will be paid to solve in meeting the principal responsibilities of the job.

You should find the following exercise helpful in defining and profiling core job knowledge.

Defining Core Knowledge

1. What the key *functions* performed or managed by this position?

2. What are the key, ongoing functional *accountabilities* of the job (i.e., the key "results" expected for each function for which the job is responsible)?

3. What are the *major problems* that must be solved in each of these areas of functional responsibility in order to achieve these desired results?

4. What *core or specialized knowledge* is required to solve these key problems and achieve the desired results?

5. Beyond the ongoing functional responsibilities of the job, with what *special projects* will this position be involved?

6. What *specific results* are expected of this position with regard to these special projects?

7. What *key problems* must be solved in order to get these results?

8. What *core or specialized knowledge* is needed to solve these problems and achieve the expected results?

9. Based upon the strategic goals of the organization, what are the *major strategic changes* that this position must drive in order to assist the organization in meeting its strategic objectives?

10. What *key problems* must be solved in order to bring these strategic changes about?

11. What *core or specialized* knowledge is required to successfully solve these problems and bring the desired strategic changes about?

This exercise forces you to focus on three components that are generic elements of practically all jobs. These components are ongoing job accountabilities, project accountabilities, and strategic change accountabilities. The process that I have presented, in the form of the above exercise, allows you to define the "core knowledge" that will be required in order to meet the overall accountabilities of the job and achieve a high level of job performance.

At this point, record the core knowledge that you have identified as critical to successful job performance in the circle that you previously drew and which has been labeled "Job Fit." You are now ready to evaluate the second important dimension of job fit—motivation to perform.

PROFILING PERFORMANCE MOTIVATION

Although you may have sufficient core knowledge to meet the technical requirements of the job, an equally important question is, "Will you be sufficiently motivated by the work environment to want to perform the job?" Being "able" to perform and "wanting" to perform are two entirely different matters. Both the ability to perform and the desire to perform are required if performance success and job satisfaction are to be realized.

The nature of the work environment has much to do with motivation to perform the job. It is not only "what" you do, but "how you do it" that, together, determine the degree to which you are motivated to do the job. The nature of the work environment (i.e., the systems that govern how work is to be performed) is thus a factor which you need to carefully consider when evaluating the fit of a given employment opportunity.

In his book, *Managing Strategic Change*, Noel M. Tichy suggests that one way to gain an understanding of the work environment is to study its business systems. (Tichy's term is "technical systems.") The business system of an organization is the system by which the assets of the organization (i.e., capital, raw materials, equipment, technology, and people) are organized and managed in order to achieve the strategic objectives (short and long-term) and mission of the business. These business systems provide some strong clues about the nature of the work environment, what resources will be at your disposal, how they may be used, and so on.

The diagnostic basis for understanding an organization's business system (and therefore the profile of "high performers" in that system), is the examination of the management structure and processes used by the organization to manage its resources. This diagnosis is best accomplished through the analysis and profiling of the following key elements which are integral components of the business system:

1. Mission and strategy

2. Communication/clarity of mission and strategy

3. Organizational structure

4. Performance standards (business units and individuals)

5. Key problems and issues (internal and external)

6. Resource planning and allocation process

7. Needs of internal/external customers

8. Policies and procedures

9. Management controls.

All of these elements serve to define how work is done in the organization (i.e., the work environment), and will cumulatively impact your motivation to do the job.

Let's now examine the nature of the work environment by using the following exercise to profile the business or technical system of the target organization you are considering for employment. The results of this exercise should be recorded (below the core knowledge data that you have already recorded) on the "Job Profile" chart that you are developing as part of the overall "organizational profile."

Again, the questions contained in this exercise need to be incorporated into your interview plan, so that you will have the information that you will need to complete this important component of the organizational profile and arrive at an intelligent and reasoned employment decision.

Defining the Business System

1. What is the overall mission and strategy of the organization?

2. How clearly defined and understood is the mission of the organization?

3. Which of the following most drives the organization and accounts for its success?

    a. Technology

    b. Marketing

    c. Service

    d. Manufacturing expertise

    e. Reputation

    f. Name

    g. Other (Describe).

4. Which best describes the way in which the organization is structured:

    a. Vertical alignment—many levels in chain-of-command

    b. Horizontal alignment—flat with broad span of control.

5. Does the current structure align well with its strategy and mission? Why?

6. If it doesn't align well, where are the problems? Why?

7. What does the organization consider to be the two most important resources for its success?

    a. Raw materials

    b. Capital

    c. Equipment

    d. People

    e. Technology

    f. Innovation/creativity

    g. Information systems.

8. Which are the two least important resources to organizational success? Why?

    a. Raw Materials

    b. Capital

    c. Equipment

    d. People

    e. Technology

    f. Innovation/Creativity

    g. Information Systems.

9. What are the three major external threats to organizational success and survival?

10. What is the organization's strategy for meeting these threats?

11. What are the three major internal threats to organizational success and survival?

12. What is the organization's current strategy for addressing these threats?

13. What is the basis for measuring and rewarding the performance of organizational units?

14. What is the basis for measuring and rewarding the performance of individuals?

15. How does management go about controlling the organization?

    a. What 3 or 4 key factors are monitored?

    b. What 3 or 4 controls does management use?

16. What is the primary process for planning and allocating organizational resources?

    a. What is the process?

    b. Who participates in the process?

    c. How are conflicts resolved?

17. To what degree have policies, procedures, and standards been developed for management and control of the business?

    a. High Degree—Cover most situations

    b. Moderate Degree—Sufficient to cover key areas

    c. Low degree—Insufficient to cover key areas

    d. Nonexistent

18. What processes exist for planning and developing the organization's human resources?

19. How would you best classify the overall business strategy of the organization?

    a. Start-up

    b. Turnaround

    c. Dynamic Growth—Existing Business

    d. Extract Pro-rationalize—Existing Business

    e. Redeployment of Efforts—Existing Business

    f. Liquidation/Divestiture of Poorly Performing Units

    g. New Acquisitions.

As you can see, these questions can be used by you in the interview, and during the research stage of your job hunting process, to gain a considerable amount of information about the nature of the work environment in which you will be spending your time. Examining the nature of the work environment, as categorized by its business systems, can provide you with an excellent basis for determining whether work climate will be one that you will find to be motivating or demotivating. This, in turn, will greatly impact the degree of contentment you will experience in working in such a work environment and thereby determine your ultimate happiness.

We have now concluded the "Job Profile" of the organizational model. If you have diligently carried out each step of this process, you have now constructed a rather complete profile of the job in terms of its "core knowledge" and "work environment." This should enable you to determine whether you can "do the job," and whether you will be "motivated to do it." We now need to take a look at the subject of organizational compatibility.

PROFILING ORGANIZATIONAL COMPATIBILITY

As pointed out in Chapter 2 of this book, compatibility with the culture of an organization is a critical component of job success and happiness. As evidence of this, somewhere in the range of 70 to 92 percent of all professional and managerial involuntary employment terminations (i.e., firings) are not the result of technical incompetence but are, instead, caused by incompatibility with the organization's cultural.

Thus, although you may be highly technically competent and able to successfully meet the technical demands of the job (i.e., possess the core knowledge and are motivated to perform), if your personal values and belief system (and therefore your behavior) do not align well with the core value and belief system of the organization, there is a very highly likelihood for job failure and much unhappiness on your part. This is just another way of saying that it is not only "what" you do, but "how you do it" that will ultimately determine job success (and therefore happiness).

Behavioral scientists have long known that a person's behavior is driven by their value/belief systems. How a person "feels" and what a person "believes" about something, will determine how they will behave. Organizations are no different. Because the whole (the organization) is the sum of its parts (the employees), an organization's culture is defined by its core value/belief systems (i.e., those values and beliefs commonly shared by the majority of employees). As with the individual, the behavior of the organization is also driven by this core value/belief system.

Individuals whose value/belief systems do not align well with that of the organization, are thus unlikely to behave or perform in a manner which the organization feels is acceptable. Because their value/belief systems are different from that of the organizations, such employees are often seen as argumentive, rebellious, nonconforming, not a team player, a loner, and the like. Persons who are perceived this way by the organization are unlikely to get the necessary support for their ideas nor the resources necessary to succeed. Instead, such individuals will normally find themselves on the peripheral of the work group feeling isolated and alone. This isolation will eventually destroy any real motivation that the employee has to do the work and eventually the resulting drop in productivity will result in a "performance" termination.

To understand and profile organizational culture, therefore, there are three dimensions that you will need to study and then profile. These are:

1. Core values (commonly held values)

2. Core beliefs (commonly held beliefs)

3. Acceptable/Preferred behaviors.

By defining these three dimensions, you have the basis for constructing a valid model of the organization's culture, which can then be used as the basis for predicting the degree of organizational compatibility.

The degree of cultural fit has a direct relationship to how well your personal value/belief system (and therefore behavior) aligns with the core value/belief system (and therefore the behavioral norms) of the employer you are considering. If there is an exceptionally close alignment, there is a very high likelihood of a successful marriage. If the alignment is poor, divorce will shortly follow the honeymoon.

You will find the following exercise extremely helpful in defining the cultural profile of the organization. To continue with your development of the "organizational model," at this point, you will need to construct a large circle on a second piece of white paper and label this sheet "Organizational Profile." Results of this exercise are to be summarized and recorded in the form of descriptive "bullet statement" in the circle that you have drawn.

Profiling Organizational Culture
(Measuring Organizational Values and Beliefs)

1. What are the two or three things that the organization most *values* and considers important to its success?

2. Which of the following resources does the organization *believe* are most important to its success?

   a. Capital
   b. Raw Materials
   c. Equipment
   d. Technology
   e. People

3. Which does the organization *feel* are the two most important? Why?

4. Which does the organization *feel* are the least important? Why?

5. What does the organization *believe* to be the two biggest problems standing in the way of its success?

6. How does the organization rank their importance and why?

7. What are the three management attributes considered most important to organizational success? Why?

8. What three words best describes the organization's preferred management philosophy? Why?

9. What three words best depict the management operating style most preferred by the company?

10. From a "quality of work life" standpoint, what are the five most positive aspects of working in the organization?

11. How would the organization rank these? Why?

12. What words best describe the organization's approach to training and development?

13. What words best describe the organization's approach to employee career development?

14. What five words best describe the organization's public image or reputation?

15. What criteria are most frequently used by the organization as the basis for compensation and rewards?

Profiling High Performers
(Profiling Organizational Values & Beliefs)

1. What personal traits or characteristics set "high performers" apart from others in this organization?

2. How are "high performers" in this organization categorized in terms of their business philosophy (i.e., what they believe to be important to organizational success)?

3. How does the organization describe these same "high performers" from the standpoint of their operating style (i.e., how they go about doing their work)?

4. In general, what type of behavior tends to be well recognized and rewarded by the organization?

As you can readily see, both of the previous exercises will provide you with considerable insight regarding the core values and beliefs of the organization. These core values and beliefs can be "directly" identified by asking some fairly direct questions or identified "indirectly" by observing how an organization behaves (i.e., what it does) with respect to a given area which is important to your personal job and career satisfaction.

Having completed these exercises, you will now want to record your observations about the organizational culture on the "Organizational Profile" sheet which you previously prepared. I would suggest recording these observations (in brief bullet statements) within the circle and under the subheading of "Organizational Culture."

Although we have examined and profiled the organizational culture of the target organization as part of our overall "organizational model," another important dimension that you need to consider in completing your model are the social and political systems of the organization. This will be our next step.

PROFILING SOCIAL AND POLITICAL SYSTEMS

Noel Tichy, in this book, *Managing Strategic Change,* points out that besides the culture of the organization, there are also the social and political systems of the organization that are important to categorizing the nature of an organization. Understanding these organizational systems is also extremely important to predicting a successful marriage from the employment perspective. If one does not align well with these two systems, he or she will be powerless and unable to perform effectively within the organizational environment.

Alignment with the social and political system will thus be critical to your ability to perform in the organization. This will directly affect the probability for successful performance and therefore your organizational fit and job satisfaction. Good employment decisions will therefore require careful evaluation of such a fit.

The social and political system are the sources of formal and informal power, authority, and control of the organization and thus have considerable impact on the nature and characteristics of the organization's work environment.

For purposes of understanding, the following is the distinction between the "social" and the "political" systems of an organization.

1. *Social System:* The social system is the "informal" network or alliance of interpendent persons (often but not always at the same organizational level) who group together as a result of common interests. Although they do not not have true power or authority in the formal organizational sense, they have the ability (through their organizational

connections) to significantly influence the organization's decision-making process and, therefore, the behavioral norms of the organization (i.e., how things get done).

2. *Political System:* The political system of an organization is the "formal" alliance of persons (usually as defined by the organization chart or similar formal, sanctioned alliance) who have the "formal" responsibility and authority for decision-making. It is the formal relationship by which one individual (or group) within the organization exercises power and control over another individual (or group).

The social and political systems of the organization have enormous impact on the way work is done (and decisions are made) in the organization. They basically define the decision-making environment and provide strong clues about the human traits, characteristics, and behaviors that are required to be effective in a given work environment.

For example, a highly structured work environment (e.g., rigid, well-defined organization chart; strong top-down decision-making process; well-defined policies and procedures; close supervision and strong management controls) would hardly be a good match if you are someone who dislikes functional boundaries, likes to push the outer limits, enjoys independent decision making and freedom, is highly entrepreneurial, enjoys risk-taking, etc. In such a case, you would be at odds with the organization's social and political systems (the sources of power and control) and would be totally powerless and ineffective.

The basis for understanding and profiling an organization's political and social systems is to study the power structure of the organization. This is best understood by examining how decisions get made in the organization (i.e., the decision making process). By defining "who" makes decisions and "how" different kinds of decisions get made, you can better understand and gauge the balance of power between the social (informal) system and the political (formal) system.

It is important to understand that the skill set for successful performance in an organization that relies heavily on its social system for decision making is very different from the skill set required for successful performance in a work environment that relies heavily on its political system for decision making. To ensure a good organizational fit, therefore, it is important to be sure that your personal traits, characteristics, style and preferences align well with the predominant power system of the organization that you are considering for employment.

The following exercise will help you to understand and profile a target organization from the standpoint of its balance between social and political power, thus providing a vital element in the overall "organizational model" that you are constructing. Here again, you will want to be sure to address these questions at the time of your employment interview (or during the research portion of your job search), so that you have the information available to complete this exercise and construct the organizational model.

Profiling Social/Political Systems

1. How is the organization structured?
   - a. By function
   - b. By product line
   - c. By business area/unit
   - d. Other (Describe)

2. Which best describes the overall nature of the organization?
   - a. Centralized—strong central control
   - b. Decentralized—autonomous decision making

3. What is the overall process for planning and allocating resources?
   - a. How is planning done?
   - b. Who participates?

    c. How are final decisions made?

    d. Who makes final decisions?

4. To what degree does *senior level management* get involved with decision making at various levels of the organization? (Code: High degree—moderate degree—seldom—never)

    a. Defining long-term goals

    b. Determining long-term strategies & plans

    c. Defining intermediate-term goals

    d. Determining intermediate-term strategies & plans

    e. Defining short-term goals

    f. Determining short-term strategies and plans

    g. Determining day-to-day operating decisions

5. To what degree does *middle level management* tend to get involved with various levels of decision making? (Use same code as in # 4 above)

    a. Defining long-term goals

    b. Determining long-term strategies and plans

    c. Defining intermediate-term goals

    d. Determining intermediate-term strategies and plans

    e. Defining short-term goals

    f. Determining short-term strategies and plans

    g. Determining day-to-day operating decisions

6. How do decisions get made when contingencies or crises arise?

7. When conflict arises in a work team or functional area, how does it get resolved?

8. How, how often, and what does senior management communicate about organizational strategy and organizational progress to employees?

9. Using the following codes, in general how does the organization rank the importance of each of the following to the basic, day-to-day decision-making process? (Code: major importance—moderate importance—little or no importance)

    a. Policies & procedures

    b. Defined authority

    c. Negotiations between parties

    d. Social/Political networks

10. When disputes erupt between functional areas of the organization, which best describes how they are normally resolved?

    a. Chain-of-command

    b. Employee negotiations

11. Below the management level, which best describes what the nature of the working relations is between employees in various departments?

    a. Little or no interaction

    b. Occasional work interaction

    c. Moderate work interaction

    d. Frequent & close interaction

12. To what degree does the organization use matrix (vs. chain-of-command) management?

    a. Little or no use of matrix management

    b. Occasional use of matrix management

    c. Moderate or regular use of matrix management

    d. Continuous or frequent use of matrix management

13. Which word best describes the predominant management style of the organization when making business decisions?

    a. Participative—Input from employees

    b. Group Consensus—Management by committees or groups

    c. Autocratic—Management by a select few

    d. Authoritarian—Management by a single authority

14. Which word best categorizes the organization's decision-making process?

    a. Formal—Well structured and clearly defined

    b. Informal—Unstructured and loosely defined

15. Which would employees below the management level select to describe their ability to impact the organization?

    a. Great impact—plenty of opportunity to input and influence how things are done

    b. High impact—a good deal of opportunity to input and influence how things are done

    c. Moderate impact—ample opportunity to input and influence how things are done

    d. Little impact—most decisions made by management, little opportunity to input and influence how things are done

    e. No impact—no opportunity to input and influence how things are done

16. Which of the options contained in #15 above would middle management choose to best describe their impact on the organization?

As you can see, use of the above questions will enable you to obtain a very accurate profile of the power structure of the organization and the manner in which decision-making occurs. From this you can deduce whether the balance of the power is with the social or the political systems of the organization. These decision-making characteristics of the organization which you have identified through the use of this exercise can now be incorporated into your "organizational model."

These power and decision-making characteristics should be recorded (in short bullet type statements) in the circle contained on your "Organizational Profile." Use the subheading "Social and Political Systems."

You have now completed the "Organizational Profile" portion of the organizational model that you are constructing for employment decision-making purposes. The next component of the overall organization model is "compatibility with business strategy."

PROFILING BUSINESS STRATEGY

Studies done by Marc Gerstein and Heather Reisman ("Strategic Selection: Matching Executives to Business Systems," *Sloan Management Review,* Winter 1983), show that there is a strong linkage between an organization's business strategy and the skills and attributes needed to successfully perform against such strategy. Hence, in evaluating your probability for a good fit with a given employer, you will need to ascertain the overall business strategy of the organization and determine whether or not you have the requiste skills and characteristics known to be important to successful performance and overall job satisfaction. As you will recall, much of this has already been discussed in Chapter 2 of this book.

For this next exercise, you will want to refer to the seven different business strategies and corresponding list of key skills (as defined in the Gerstein and Resiman study) provided for each strategy as set forth in Chapter 2. Use these strategy descriptions and corresponding key skill listings to do the following:

Profiling Business Strategy & Key Skills

1. Choose the business strategy that best categorizes the current strategy of your target employer (see Chapter 2, pages 26–28). Choices are:

    a. Start-up

    b. Turnaround

    c. Extract Profit/Rationalize Existing Business

    d. Dynamic Growth in Existing Business

    e. Redeployment of Efforts in Existing Business

    f. Liquidation/Divestiture of Poorly Performing Business Units

    g. New Acquisitions

2. List the key skills required for successful performance in each of these strategic environments.

Both the strategy category chosen to best describe the target organization and the corresponding key skill and attribute set should be recorded on a separate sheet of white paper entitled "Strategic Compatibility Profile." This sheet should now be added to the rest of the overall "organizational model" that you have constructed.

PROFILING NEW BOSS

The traits and characteristics of a boss can have significant impact on your motivation and attitude toward the job. If the two of you align well philosophically and your styles are compatible, there will normally be a great deal of harmony, and you will thoroughly enjoy your working relationship. Conversely, if your value/belief systems and styles are very different, chances are there will be constant friction and a good deal of stress in your life.

Being compatible with your new boss will thus play a critical role in your ability to perform the job and in your overall job satisfaction and career happiness. It is important then, as a part of the predictive modeling process that you gain some insight regarding the characteristics of what might become your next boss. The following exercise will help you to accomplish this.

Profiling the Perspective New Boss

1. How would you describe the business philosophy of the new boss (i.e., what he/she believes is important to organizational success)?

2. How would you categorize the management philosophy of the new boss (i.e., what he/she believes is important to effective management)?

3. Describe the operating style of the new boss (i.e., the way in which he/she likes to perform his/her work)?

4. What management styles and techniques does the new boss like to employ when managing subordinates?

6. What are the 3 or 4 most important criteria used by the new boss to gauge work performance?

7. Which is the most important? Why?

8. Which are the least important? Why?

9. What factors does the new boss feel are least relevant to job performance? Why?

10. How does the new boss handle the planning process? To what degree are subordinates involved?

11. What basis and techniques does this new boss use to manage and control the volume and quality of a subordinate's work? Why?

12. To what degree does the new boss like to be involved in day-to-day operations? Why?

13. What kinds of decisions will you be encouraged to make vs those that the new boss wishes to reserve for himself/herself? Why?

14. How do conflicts in the immediate work group get resolved?

15. What is the process for allocating resources within the workgroup.

As can be seen, answers to these and similar questions will do a great deal to profile the characteristics of the new boss as an important component of your "organizational model." You will have a good understanding of the values, beliefs, management behavior, and so on, of this important person. Direct comparison of this component of the organizational model with the "Best Boss" component of your "personal predictive model" (see Chapter 2) will go a long way to assist you in accurately gauging and predicting the degree of compatibility (or incompatibility) with this potential new boss—and therefore, will contribute to an intelligent employment decision.

THE PREDICTION

Whew!! Well, after a rather lengthy but worthwhile journey, we have concluded the final component of the organizational model. At this point, your organizational model should be comprised of the following documents and components:

1. Job Profile
   a. Core Knowledge & Skills Summary
   b. Motivation to Perform Summary
   c. Business Systems Summary

2. Organizational Profile
   a. Core Values & Beliefs Summary
   b. "High Performer" Summary
   c. Social & Political Systems Summary

3. Strategic Compatibility Profile

4. New Boss Profile

You now are in possession of a very complete profile of the target organization and all of the key elements that are known to be critical to a good fit from a job performance and compatibility standpoint. The "organizational model" that you have developed now becomes the target against which you will need to compare the "predictive model" which you developed back in Chapter 2 of this book.

By laying these two models side-by-side and comparing one against the other, you will readily see whether or not the target job and organization are going to be a good match for your knowledge, skills, and personal traits & characteristics. Your predictive model thus becomes an excellent tool for predicting, with a high degree of accuracy, just how good a match it will really be.

Finally, it is important to understand that no job or organization is going to be a perfect fit for your specific predictive model profile. In final analysis, therefore, intelligent job selection boils down to a matter of risk analysis and risk management. The remaining questions that you will need to ask yourself prior to making that final decision are:

1. In what areas do my personal predictive model not fit the organizational model?

2. Will these elements be critical to successful job performance and career happiness?

3. What do these gaps suggest about areas I will need to pay particular attention to from a job performance and development standpoint?

4. What development plans can I put into place to enable me to close these gaps?

5. What adjustments am I going to need to make in my value/belief system and behavior in order to be compatible with the culture of the organization?

6. How critical are these shifts, and can I make them?

7. What is my plan for making these modifications?

These and similar questions will go a long way to evaluating the degree of risk involved in accepting a given job offer and to selecting jobs and work environments in which you will be both highly productive and generally happy.

14

Negotiating the Job Offer

This chapter deals with the subject of negotiating the job offer. If you are to bring your job search to an acceptable conclusion, you must learn to be a skillful negotiator. Lack of good negotiating skills is critical at this phase of the job search process, and could cause all of your hard work to be for nothing, should you fail. Failure can result from receiving an unacceptable offer or from scaring the employer away with what might be considered unreasonable demands. Both situations are avoidable with a little advance planning and strategy.

This chapter will provide you with some basic strategy that should prove helpful in designing and executing effective job offer negotiations. It will give you a basis for determining a fair offer amount, and for effective presentation of this information to the employer. Likewise, it will explore the offer from the employer's standpoint and provide you with insight concerning the factors that tend to shape the employer's thinking when formulating an employment offer. Having this broad understanding should be helpful in formulating an offer strategy that will contribute to achievement of successful results for both parties.

DETERMINING THE EMPLOYER'S LIMITS

The first step in formulating an effective negotiation strategy is to determine the salary range within which the employer must operate. It is very important, where possible, to establish these limitations in advance of the actual negotiation process.

Most companies will not make an offer at, or near, the top of the salary range for the position. If they do, you should have some concern. Specifically, how is this going to affect your future salary treatment? Chances are, not too well.

If you are dealing with a third party (i.e., employment agency or executive search firm), the job of finding out the salary range of the position will likely be a bit easier. Most, if they know, will share this information with you; but you've got to ask them for it. Some executive search firms, because they have been retained by the employer, may be unwilling to disclose this information on the basis that it may prejudice the negotiating process. For example, if the salary range of the position is $80,000 to $110,000 and you are now earning $70,000, knowing the range maximum may cause you to ask for considerably more than you would have otherwise.

The fact that some of these firms may be unwilling to provide you with salary range information should not stop you from asking. Since this is vital to your negotiating strategy, you shouldn't hesitate to ask. In most cases you will find that these firms, in the interest of putting the deal together, will be willing to share this information with you. If, for some reason, they are unaware of what the salary range is, ask them to find out.

Where there is no third party involved in the process, or where the third party is unwilling to disclose the salary range, you may need to secure this data from the employer directly. In such cases, the employer may be somewhat reluctant to share this information on the basis that you will use it to improve your own negotiating position. Although this strikes to the truth of the matter, the employer can usually be made to feel a little more comfortable with your request, if it is properly positioned. Here is a tactic that you might try:

> Jane, what is the salary range for this position? I would prefer to avoid the situation where I might be hired near or at the range maximum. My experience has been that being compensated at this level frequently leads to future salary administration problems, making it difficult to be appropriately compensated for above average or outstanding performance. Such a situation would concern me.

This type of request seems quite reasonable and will usually elicit a fairly direct response from the employer. On the other hand, some employers have a policy that prohibits disclosure of salary range information to employees. (Fortunately, such companies are in the minority.) If this is the case, however, and the company representative is unwilling to disclose salary facts, here is another strategy that you might employ:

> Look, Jane, I can appreciate that it is against company policy to disclose salary range information, and I don't want to make you uncomfortable with this request. I'm sure, however, that you can appreciate my concerns, as well. Maybe there is a creative solution to this. Perhaps, without disclosing the actual range, you can tell me where my current salary is, relative to the total range. For example, in which quartile does it fall—first, second, third or fourth? Approximately where would it be slotted?

This is a reasonable request, and you have provided good grounds for wanting to know this information. Considering the circumstances, and the way that you have framed your request, it would be very difficult for the company representative to continue to withhold salary information from you without risking the relationship, and potentially jeopardizing the recruiting process. If the employer has any possible interest in your candidacy, it will be most difficult to refuse your request. At this point in the process, you are still somewhat in the driver's seat and have some leverage. Once the actual negotiations start, however, it is too late to request this information, and would be inappropriate to do so.

Now that you have acquired some information concerning the salary range, you are in a more informed position to formulate a successful negotiating strategy. Without this, you have no basis for intelligently pegging a sensible compensation figure, and you are totally at the mercy of the employer.

When formulating your salary request, it is important to realize that employers, for the most part, prefer to make offers that are at, or below, the salary range midpoint. In this way, they can provide the new hire with ample room for salary growth, based upon performance and contribution, and not have to worry about future salary administration problems. The higher in the range they must go to attract a suitable candidate, the greater is the concern for future salary administration issues. This is particularly true when there is no identifiable promotional opportunity to which the candidate can be promoted short range. The higher your current salary is in relationship to the employer's salary range, therefore, the more you may want to shave the amount of increase that you are requesting. If you are too high in the range, and are requesting too much, you could price yourself out of the market, and no offer may be forthcoming.

If, on the other hand, you are at or below the minimum of the employer's salary range, you have considerably more latitude. Percentage wise, in this case, you will want to ask for a substantial salary increase, realizing the employer can afford to be flexible. If you are extremely well-qualified, employers will wish to avoid the possibility of some other company sweeping you away with a better offer in the future. There is, therefore, added incentive for the employer to increase the ante. This is especially true if you are in a high demand discipline.

Position in salary range is a factor that has significant influence on what the employer is willing to offer in the way of compensation. Although salary range is, by far, the most significant factor affecting the employer's decision, you need to be aware that there are several other factors as well. Let's take a look at some of these.

OTHER FACTORS AFFECTING COMPENSATION

On the employer's side of the equation, there are a number of factors, other than salary range, that will impact the salary amount offered to a successful candidate. These factors are:

1. Internal salary equity

2. Availability of other qualified candidates

3. Difficulty in filling position

4. Length of time position has been open

5. Criticalness of filling position

6. Level of interest in candidate

7. Candidate's level of interest

8. Availability of future promotional opportunities

9. Candidate's potential for future promotion.

Internal salary equity refers to the relationship of the candidate's salary to the members of the existing work group who are at the same level. Employers are concerned with hiring outsiders at significantly higher compensation levels than members of the current work group, unless such differential is justified on the basis of qualifications and experience level. It would be difficult, for example, to hire a Ph.D. with four years experience, at $75,000, if the other Ph.D.s in the group average six years of experience and are making only $65,000. To do so would cause a serious inequity, and create the potential for dissension should the other work group members discover this fact. In preparing your negotiating strategy, you should be aware of the backgrounds and experience levels of your peer group, and should take time to estimate their probable earnings levels.

Another factor affecting the employer's decision on compensation is the difficulty in filling the position. If there is a healthy supply of qualified candidates on the market and the position has only been open for a short period, you should assume that the employer will be less receptive to a large increase over your current salary level. If there are very few qualified persons available and the position has been open for a long time, the employer may be more flexible on the salary issue. During the interview, therefore, you should attempt to get a feel for this. Here are some questions to use in acquiring this information:

1. How long has this position been open?

2. How many candidates have you interviewed?

3. How many candidates are you actively considering?

4. By when would you expect to be making an offer on this position?

5. How important is it to fill this position shortly?

Answers to questions such as these can go a long way toward telling you how well you stack up against the competition, or if there is any competition at all. Obviously, the less the competition and the greater the need to fill the position, the more flexible the employer is likely to be on salary. Conversely, the stiffer the competition and the less the urgency to fill the position, the less flexible the employer will be on the subject of compensation. You need to get a good fix on these factors when formulating your offer strategy.

Interest level is also a factor in determining one's negotiating strategy. The stronger the employer's interest in the candidate, the higher the offer amount that the candidate can usually command. Conversely, the lower the interest level of the employer, the lower will be the offer. You must be attentive to the employer's interest level in you.

Another factor that influences the employer's decision on salary offer is the degree of job interest shown by the candidate. If the candidate is clearly excited about the position and communicates this to the employer, the employer will likely shave the offer a bit. On the other hand, where the candidate has expressed interest in the position, but implied that he or she was also considering other things, the employer may be more prone to go in with a higher offer amount in an effort to cement the deal. As part of your negotiation strategy, therefore, you will want to keep your powder dry. Express interest in the position, but don't telegraph your excitement, if you want to get the employer's highest offer. On the other hand, if the competition is stiff and you really want the job, by all means, express your excitement and enthusiasm for the position. In this case, getting a slightly lower offer is well worth assuring yourself a job offer.

Promotability is also a factor affecting compensation level. If the candidate appears to have good potential for promotion beyond the current job, and should a promotional opportunity be readily identifiable, the employer will usually be a little more lenient about compensation. In such cases, the employer will have little concern about making an offer that is high in the salary range. On the other hand, should the candidate have excellent promotional potential, and should there be no identifiable position available for future promotion, the employer will tend to shave the offer, hoping to forestall future salary administration problems. Likewise, if the candidate should appear to have little promotability potential beyond the position for which he or she would be hired, the employer will normally opt for more conservative salary treatment. The employer is concerned about having enough room in the current salary range to keep the new hire satisfied for a fairly long period of time.

There are several factors besides salary range that must be taken into consideration when determining your negotiating strategy. You should carefully think your way through each of these factors before deciding on your target compensation level for negotiation purposes. Judicious consideration of these factors, along with the salary range information that you previously collected, should leave you with a fairly good insight on how the employer is likely to view the structuring of the employment offer. This should help you to zero in on the maximum amount the employer is likely to offer. The other side of the equation is determining the minimum amount that you are willing to accept.

YOUR ROCK-BOTTOM PRICE

Once you have estimated the maximum amount the employer is likely to offer, the next step in preparing your negotiation strategy is to determine the minimum salary that you would be willing to accept. Although in rare cases you might be willing to accept a salary reduction for a given job, usually you are looking for an increase in compensation level. The theory here is that, in addition to increasing the satisfaction derived from *psychic* income, most persons are looking to increase *capital* income, as well.

It should be pointed out that an increase in gross income does not, in itself, assure an increase in net disposable income (i.e., actual buying power). There are, in fact, a number of cost variables that can convert what appears on the surface to be a gain, into an actual loss of substantial proportions. This is particularly so when one is relocating to a new area in order to accept the job. Without some careful analysis, you can be in for a rude awakening.

The key to understanding whether a given offer is financially attractive, requires you to make a comparison between net disposable income in the old job and location with net disposable income in the new job and location. A simple comparison of gross income amounts, unfortunately, won't suffice.

In order to facilitate a comparison, consider the formula shown on the forms at the end of this chapter. This formula should be used twice—once to calculate current net disposable income in the current job and location, and second, to calculate net disposable income in the new job and location. Comparing these two net disposable income amounts should provide you with a determination of your actual gains or losses in accepting a given employment offer.

In applying this formula, there are a few subtleties to keep in mind:

1. Both state and local income taxes are deductible from federal income tax. The number used for federal income tax in this formula must be adjusted accordingly.

2. Mortgage interest, real estate tax, personal property tax, state excise tax, and state sales tax may also be deductible from federal income taxes. Check with your tax advisor, and adjust the federal tax calculated in this formula.

3. To reflect an accurate housing comparison, you must adjust your new location housing costs to reflect comparable housing size in your new location. Thus, if you now have a 2,500 square foot house in your current location, the new housing costs must also reflect the cost of a similar 2,500 square foot house in the new location. Contact with two or three realtors in the new location should help you get realistic estimates. (Note: The new employer should not be expected to help you finance the cost of a larger house. All calculations should therefore be based upon the same size and style house in both locations.)

By experimenting with different gross income figures and using the formula supplied at the end of the chapter, it should be possible for you to determine the amount of gross salary increase that will be required for you to break even or show some improvement in net disposable income. Because of the potential for significant variation in cost of living factors between different locations, however, it is very important for you to go through this analysis in advance of negotiating your offer. If you find these costs are significantly higher in the new location, you have some fairly powerful ammunition to support your increased salary demands during the negotiation process. On the other hand, if the cost of living in the new location is significantly less than the old location, you may find that little or no increase in gross income will be necessary for you to improve your net disposable income and increase your purchasing power.

This calculation should provide you with useful insight regarding the amount of the offer that you will require as rock-bottom to make this particular move financially palatable.

ACTUAL NEGOTIATIONS

You should now have a good idea of the maximum amount that the employer will be willing to offer. You also know your own rock-bottom price, as well.

At the beginning of actual negotiations, you will likely be asked to indicate the level of offer that you are looking for. In all cases you should respond with an amount that you believe to be slightly in excess of the maximum amount that you believe they are prepared to offer. In this way, you have allowed sufficient room for negotiations.

When responding to this request, it is usually a good idea to provide some underlying rationale for the amount that you are requesting. This way, you don't appear as though you are being arbitrary. Such rationale could be as follows:

> Sam, although it may, at first, seem a little high, I feel that I'm going to need an offer of about $95,000 to make this interesting.

Some research that I have done on cost of living differential between here and Chicago suggests that I will need another $6,000 in gross income just to break even. Since this position represents an increase in accountability over my past job, I would also like to see some increase in overall income, in the neighborhood of $5,000. I am thus requesting a total increase of $11,000, taking my salary from $84,000 to $95,000. Backing out cost of living differential, this represents an increase of only $5,000 or 6.0 percent, which to me seems reasonable. What do you think?

Notice how effectively the cost of living data was used. In addition, because of the detailed prepared analysis, you are ready to substantiate your claims regarding living costs. You are pointing out that your real gain is only 6.0 percent versus the 13 percent suggested by the overall $11,000 increase. The distinction, of course, is the difference in cost of living between your current community and that of Chicago. This makes the request appear considerably more compatible than had you offered no rationale for the compensation request.

Should the employer indicate that this is more than they are prepared to offer, you may want to qualify them further by determining how much they are willing to pay and why. Here is how that might be handled:

Employer: That's a lot more than we were thinking of.

Candidate: Well, what did you have in mind?

Employer: We were thinking of an offer in the $80,000 to $85,000 range.

Candidate: I see. Quite frankly, that's a little less than I was hoping for. Can you share with me some of your thinking behind this amount?

Employer: Well, we are concerned about creating some internal salary inequities. You see, two of our other employees, who have comparable credentials to your own, are earning $85,000. As a result, we would feel most uncomfortable going beyond the $85,000 to $87,000 range.

Candidate: Although this is a little lower than I had hoped, I can appreciate the position this puts you in. Why don't we agree to $85,000 then?

In this case, it should be evident that the employer is not prepared to go higher with its offer. The major issue here is salary inequity, and although the company may be able to tolerate a $2,000 differential, it is highly unlikely that they will risk the potential for internal unrest by going much higher. If you attempt to push the offer much higher, it is possible that you could jeopardize the whole deal.

When the employer counters with a lower offer, you should always ask why. If there is no good underlying reason for low-balling the offer, you can usually fairly safely assume that this lower offer is just a part of their negotiating strategy, and they are simply trying to get you down from your original request. In such cases, there is usually some room on the up side for you to negotiate further. Perhaps, you might suggest splitting the difference.

On the other hand, when the employer is willing to share the rationale behind a lower offer, you will want to listen carefully. Listen not only to the reason behind the lower offer, but to tone as well. If there is a good reason stated for the lower offer and the tone of the conversation suggests that the employer is fairly determined about this, then there is little likelihood that there is room for further negotiations. You can usually assume that you are already at their maximum number and the probability is high that you will kill negotiations if you try to push things much further.

In summary then, the basic rules to remember when negotiating an offer are:

1. Determine position salary range.

2. Be alert to other factors that could affect the amount the employer is willing to offer.

3. Based on the first two items, try to estimate the maximum amount the employer is likely to offer.

4. Determine through careful analysis, including cost of living factors, the minimum amount you are prepared to accept.

5. Always request slightly more than you believe the employer is prepared to offer.

6. Always provide the employer with some underlying rationale for your offer request.

7. When the employer counters with an offer that is below the level of your request, ask for the rationale. (Listen for both validity of this rationale as well as the employer's tone.)

8. When rationale for this lower offer seems somewhat weak, and the employer's tone doesn't suggest strong resolve, assume there is further room for negotiations. Either stick with your original request (if not much higher than the counter offer) or suggest an acceptable compromise figure (if there is a significant differential between your request and the counter offer).

9. When the rationale provided by the employer seems fairly solid and the employer's tone suggests a strong resolve to go no higher than the counter offer amount, it is probably unwise to attempt to negotiate further if you are truly interested in the position. You will probably want to suggest a compromise amount (probably half way between the two) just to test this resolve, but be prepared to back off quickly should the employer indicate that they have no further flexibility. At this point, you are probably at the *take it or leave it* stage.

MOVING COSTS

When negotiating with the employer, an area that may be overlooked by the inexperienced job hunter is moving expense reimbursement. If acceptance of the position will require you to relocate, this is not a consideration that you should ignore. The costs of moving can be enormous, and can prove financially devastating if not at least in part paid for by the employer. A real estate commission of 7 percent on a $200,000 home, for example, can cost you $14,000 alone. Shipment of your household goods could easily be another $6,000 to $10,000, dependent upon the size of your house and the distance of the move. Already your costs could be $20,000 to $24,000, without so much as blinking an eye.

So that you are not caught by surprise, here is a list of moving expense items for which you should be prepared to negotiate with the employer:

Moving Expense

1. Househunting trip to the new location.

2. Shipment of household goods (and storage, if necessary).

3. Temporary living expenses (while waiting to move into new quarters).

4. Double housing expense (if needing to carry mortgages and other expenses on both the old and the new location houses at the same time).

5. Third party home buying assistance (if you anticipate difficulty in selling your old location residence).

6. Reimbursement of sale closing costs (on sale of your old location house).

7. Reimbursement of purchase closing costs (on purchase of new location house).

8. Reimbursement of lease penalty fee or forfeited rent (should you be renting and need to break your lease agreement).

9. Tax gross-up for all taxable moving expenses, reimbursed to you by the employer. (Note: Certain moving expense

reimbursements constitute taxable income under federal tax laws.)

These moving expenses can be substantial. It is important, therefore, that you take time to estimate them in advance of your negotiations, so that you have some idea as to what you are dealing with in terms of total price tag. Such analysis will also serve to allow you to be more definitive when entering into discussions with the employer on this matter.

It is difficult to suggest a specific negotiating strategy for moving expense reimbursement, since there is considerable variance in what companies are willing to pay. Even within the same company, there may be considerable variance in reimbursement, dependent upon job level. It is strongly recommended, therefore, that you investigate this area thoroughly during the interview process so that you have some advance knowledge of the company's position. Here are some questions you might use:

1. What is your policy regarding moving expense reimbursement for this level position?

2. Specifically, what expenses are the company willing to reimburse?

3. What items of expense are considered to be negotiable?

4. What items are generally considered nonnegotiable? Why?

Answers to these and similar questions will go a long way toward formulating a reasonable negotiating strategy for moving expense reimbursement. Without these answers, you'll be groping in the dark.

GET IT IN WRITING

Whatever the final offer package you end up negotiating, there is one critical thing to remember: Get it in writing! There are numerous details covered verbally during the negotiating process, and sometimes people have short memories regarding the specifics of the final agreement. To avoid disagreement and potential unpleasantness, it is in your best interest to request that the employer confirm the details of the offer in writing. In this way, there can be little confusion as to what was agreed upon. This is a very reasonable request, and one that the majority of employers will willingly grant.

Net Disposable Income Comparison
(Old Location)

Gross Income (salary, bonus, other)		$_____
Less Income Taxes:		
Federal	$_____	
State	_____	
Local	_____	
Total		_____
Less Housing Costs:		
Mortgage Interest	_____	
Real Estate Taxes	_____	
Homeowners Insurance	_____	
Heat	_____	
Water	_____	
Electricity	_____	
Total		_____
Less Cost of Benefits:		
Life Insurance	_____	
Medical Insurance	_____	
Disability Insurance	_____	
Dental Insurance	_____	
Retirement Plan	_____	
Other Benefits	_____	
Total		_____

Less Miscellaneous:
    Personal Property Tax   ——————
    State Excise Tax   ——————
    State Sales Tax Estimate   ——————
    Commuting Costs   ——————
    Automobile Insurance   ——————
    Other   ——————
    Total   ——————
Less Total Expenses $——————
Net Disposable Income $——————

Net Disposable Income Comparison
(New Location)

Gross Income (salary, bonus, other) $——————
    Less Income Taxes:
        Federal $——————
        State   ——————
        Local   ——————
        Total   ——————
    Less Housing Costs:
        Mortgage Interest   ——————
        Real Estate Taxes   ——————
        Homeowners Insurance   ——————
        Heat   ——————
        Water   ——————
        Electricity   ——————
        Total   ——————
    Less Cost of Benefits:
        Life Insurance   ——————
        Medical Insurance   ——————
        Disability Insurance   ——————
        Dental Insurance   ——————
        Retirement Plan   ——————
        Other Benefits   ——————
        Total   ——————

Less Miscellaneous:

Personal Property Tax	_____
State Excise Tax	_____
State Sales Tax Estimate	_____
Commuting Costs	_____
Automobile Insurance	_____
Other	_____
Total	_____

Less Total Expenses $_____

Net Disposable Income $_____

Index